The Perfect Pond Detective Book

The Biological Balance

Peter J May

CONTENTS

Establishing your pond and adding the right ingredients.

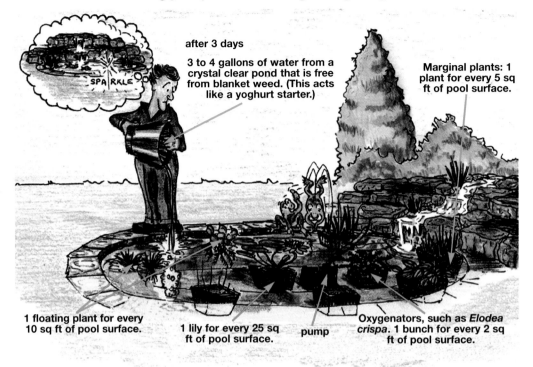

after 3 days

3 to 4 gallons of water from a crystal clear pond that is free from blanket weed. (This acts like a yoghurt starter.)

SPARKLE

Marginal plants: 1 plant for every 5 sq ft of pool surface.

1 floating plant for every 10 sq ft of pool surface.

1 lily for every 25 sq ft of pool surface.

pump

Oxygenators, such as *Elodea crispa*. 1 bunch for every 2 sq ft of pool surface.

3. It must be away from trees, particularly if prevailing winds are likely to carry poisonous leaves into the pond. As they decay in the pool, all leaves will cause some excessive load to the pool nitrogen cycle, but the leaves of willow, elder, poplar, laburnum, yew and oak are highly toxic.
4. Avoid siting the pool where there is too much exposure to the north or prevailing winds.
5. Avoid the boggy, water-logged area. It might seem the most suitable area to have a water garden but, if you use a liner in your pool, there will always be the threat of groundwater pushing up the liner from underneath. Even if you manage to puddle it and allow the water to drain away from the surrounding land to get into it in some clever way, you would then have the danger of fertilisers and other pollutants draining into it.
6. For the reason above, make sure the surrounding edge of the pool, be it paving, rock or grass, drains away from the pool.
7. Consider carefully the size and shape of the pool you want. Will all the things you want to keep in your pond fit in quite happily? (See *Stocking levels*, page 8.)

Whilst not going for the cheapest materials, make the pool as large as your pocket or energy will allow. The larger a pool or pond, the steadier is the balance that it will maintain. The absolute minimum size is 2.8 sq m (30 sq ft) with a depth of 45cm (18in). If you are planning to keep Koi carp, then you need a much bigger area. The shape should be as simple as possible. Convolutions, clever angles and large indentations can be created from the shoreline ornamentation and decoration: jetties, large marginal planting areas, beaches and so on. (See *The Perfect Pond Recipe Book*.)

8. Streams running from water recycled from the pool should not be disproportionately large in relation to the pool. Remember that a stream needs at least 0.5in of water added to its surface to get it flowing and this must come from the pool. Not only this, there is a backlog of water that seems to get hidden in the system. This can mean a considerable loss of water from the pool once the stream is in full flood. The marginal plants in particular cannot stand a radical rise and fall in water level.
9. Electrics and electrical items need to be installed to the correct national standards. Have them installed, or at least checked, by a fully-qualified electrician.

Establishing Your Pond

Your aim is to establish all the necessary ingredients for the complete cycle of life in your pond so that it can evolve into a self-sufficient little world.

If the pool is filled with fresh tap water and left to age (that is, as the purifying chemicals evaporate or drop out, the water can sustain microscopic life), then many of the necessary ingredients will eventually arrive of their own accord.

To ensure that this happens as soon as possible, in the right proportions and so that there is a good cross-section of all the right microscopic ingredients, leave the fresh water in your pool to stand for three days. Then take 13–18 litres (3–4 gal) of water from a pond that you know is evenly balanced, crystal clear and free from blanket weed. Pour this into your pool and, with the same effect as a yoghurt starter, you will find the environment will leap into action. This is good for pools with filters as well.

Stocking with plants

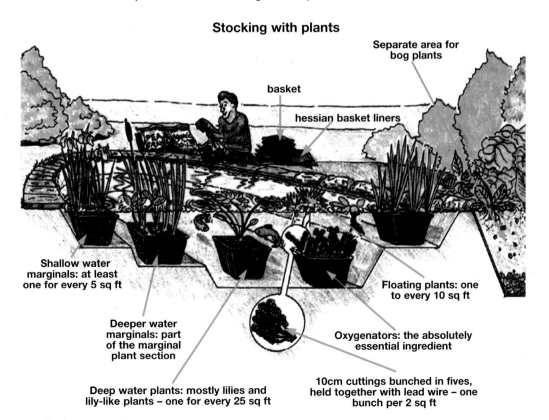

Separate area for bog plants

basket

hessian basket liners

Shallow water marginals: at least one for every 5 sq ft

Floating plants: one to every 10 sq ft

Deeper water marginals: part of the marginal plant section

Oxygenators: the absolutely essential ingredient

Deep water plants: mostly lilies and lily-like plants – one for every 25 sq ft

10cm cuttings bunched in fives, held together with lead wire – one bunch per 2 sq ft

Once the pool is full of water, in 3–10 days it will nearly always turn green. In normal circumstances just leave it with the plants in place so that the biological balance can establish itself.

Generally, after a month in the growing season, the water begins to clear. A reddish tinge is sometimes seen on the edge of the pool before it does so.

If cement lime has oozed out or run into the pond from areas you were unable to treat with Silglaze and has sent the pH up to unmanageable proportions then you have no alternative but to drain the pond and refill (see *pH,* page 32). Keep doing this until the water stays with a pH that can sustain life adequately. Plants, as well as fish, are upset by excessively limey water, but the thread algae blanket weed or Spirogyra loves a high pH, and you wouldn't want to encourage that, would you?

The Importance of Plants: the Basics
Before any animal life can arrive in your pond, you must have a cross-section of plant life settled in, ready as a welcoming party. These plants will begin to 'process' the ingredients that result from death, decay and waste matter from individuals populating the pool. Oxygenating plants will provide oxygen for the bacteria in the bottom of the pool (or filter, if you feel one is necessary) that digest waste organic matter and dead algae. These break it up gradually, eventually leaving a by-product of minerals (nitrates) that are absorbed by all the plants for growth, hopefully leaving little for the benefit of algae.

Another gain from established plants is the shade that will inhibit the growth of algae, at the same time as providing a place for the wild life of the pool to hide and spawn in.

Stocking Levels

Oxygenating plants: These are most important; without them the water will go green and stay green. Green water (see *Water Problems*, Chapter 5), although harmless in itself, is considered unsightly. It is caused by microscopic, single-celled plant life, or algae, as referred to above. Oxygenating plants can starve them out of existence by using up the light and minerals they need.

Oxygenating plants also provide the oxygen for all the life in the pool, particularly for the bacteria on the bottom of the pool that digest dead larvae, dead plant material and general excrement. Allow one bunch per 0.2 sq m (2 sq ft) of water surface.

Deep water aquatics: The most well-known of these plants is the water lily. At the height of the growing season, in order to deprive underwater algae of light and to help keep the water cool, half to two-thirds of the surface of the pool should be covered with lily pads and floating foliage.

Lilies are gross feeders and therefore do much to use excess nutrients in the pond water. This does mean that some varieties grow exceedingly quickly and are unsuitable for small pools. Allow one lily for every 2.3 sq m (25 sq ft) of pool surface.

- Take advice from a grower on suitable varieties for your pond.
- Generally, the cheaper they are, the more vigorous they are.
- Be wary of give-aways.

Floating plants: These also help to control algae by depriving them of life and using up their mineral resources. Some, such as Water Hyacinth and Water Lettuce, are frost-tender. Others, such as Water Soldier and Frogbit, sink to the bottom of the pool to avoid frost in winter. Allow one plant for every 0.9 sq m (10 sq ft) of pool surface area.

Marginal plants: These soften the edge of the pool area and use up mineral resources, especially reeds and watercress. They provide secure cover and a vegetable jetty to help wildlife in and out of the pond.

Early spring colour and the beauty of reflections come part and parcel with a certain amount of shade to the pool. The marginals also help to keep the shallow regions around the edge of the pool cool enough to stop them becoming the perfect, warm breeding ground for algae. This is the problem created by beaches, particularly if the pool becomes infested with blanket weed algae (Spirogyra).

Allow at least one plant for every 0.5 sq m (5 sq ft). Block-plant large pools or ponds. Again, be wary of give-aways.

Stocking with Fish

Allow a maximum of 1–2in of fish per square foot of surface area. It is best to transport your fish in plastic bags. When introducing fish to your pool, float the bag for 15–30

No more than 5cm (2in) of fish per square foot of the pool surface area.

Introduce several cupfuls of pool water so that the new water chemistry of the pool water does not cause stress to the fish.

Float the bag for 15 to 30 minutes in the pool so that the temperature can slowly adjust.

The rolled-down top of the plastic bag acts as a float to keep it upright.

Goldfish

Sarasa Comet

Shubunkin

Golden Orfe

Ornamental fish suitable for an outdoor pool. All are happy with each other's company.

minutes in the water so that the temperature inside the bag slowly adjusts to that of the pool. Rolling down the lip of the bag so that it forms a float keeps the bag upright.

During the time the bag is floating in the pool introduce several cupfuls of pool water so that the new water chemistry of the pool does not cause too much stress to the fish.

Apart from ordinary goldfish, other fish suitable for average pools of any size include Red Comets (Sarasas), Shubunkins, Golden Orfe, Tench and Rudd. All these will live happily with one another. More ornamental coldwater goldfish, such as bubble-eyes and fantails, find it difficult to compete with other types, particularly in the colder months. It is probably best to winter them in an indoor aquarium if you want to keep them safe and healthy.

All the above fish are quite content to share their lives with Koi carp. However, serious keepers of Koi need to think in terms of a minimum pool depth of 0.9m (3ft), and preferably 1.5–1.8m (5–6ft), with a proportionately large width and length.

Koi keepers very often have to think in terms of having no plants, or at least protecting them from the vandalism of the fish. Therefore, a sophisticated filter system is essential when keeping Koi because the biological cycle of which plants form an essential link is missing, and also because the rapid metabolism of these potentially very large fish results in a lot of waste matter. They are not fish used to extremely cold water and find our winters stressful, to say the least. When fish are stressed, they are open to disease and parasites and, since Koi are such expensive fish, the only way to keep them with confidence is to employ all the quirks of pool design and filter technology at your disposal. (See also *Adding Fish Whilst Maintaining Water Quality*, page 26.)

Wild Life

Wild pond life will generally arrive of its own free will. Very little is directly harmful to any fish or plants that you might want in the pond. In fact, it all goes into the make-up of the interdependent existence of the fabric of pond life. Watching the to-ing and fro-ing of this existence is one of the joys of owning a pool.

If wild life does not seem to be arriving soon enough, try to curb any desire to stock your pond with particular species from the wild. The exception is when a friend or neighbour wishes to donate an excess of frog or toad spawn from their urban pool; this is quite acceptable and is one way to ensure that you have a population of amphibians that will return to your pool. However, if you want to be certain that any spawn taken from the wild is not from a protected species, don't take any at all.

Freshwater shrimps, daphnia, larvae and other beasts that provide food for fishes will eventually find their own way but can be hurried along via the introduction of a few gallons of the 'starter' as described in *Establishing Your Pond*, above.

Beetles, caddisflies, skaters and dragonflies will arrive uninvited and stay if they approve. Some arrive in the mud on the roots of the plants you establish.

Wild or indigenous species of fish are best left in wild or conservation environments. Sticklebacks and minnows taken from the wild carry many pests and diseases which may be latent on them but can cause an epidemic on more 'ornamental' fish. Besides this, they can be far more aggressive than the interbred varieties, particularly when feeding, which in turn will cause stress to the domestic fish and make them susceptible to disease. (See *Conservation of 'Natural' Ponds: Choice of Fish*, page 53.)

If you already have a wild pond or conservation-style pool, the reverse is the same. Introducing domestic fish can only lead to problems that will upset the environment. (See *Conservation of 'Natural' Ponds: Choice of Fish*, page 53.)

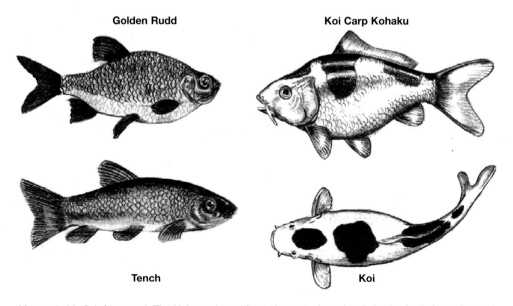

Golden Rudd　　　　　　　　　　**Koi Carp Kohaku**

Tench　　　　　　　　　　**Koi**

More suitable fish for a pool. The Koi are viewed from above to show the distinctive body formation and movements. These fish may require special conditions depending on their character and the style and space of their abode.

Spring: April to May

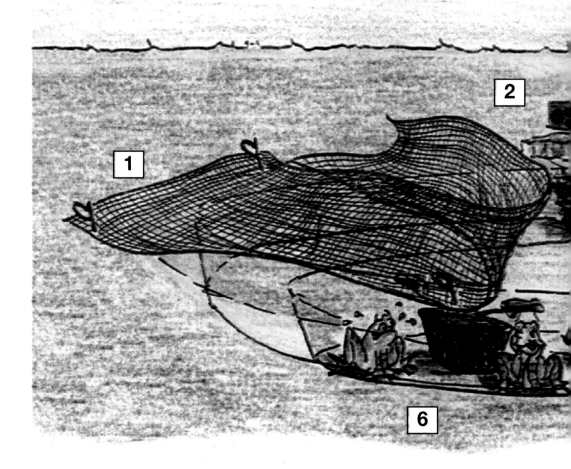

Spring: April – May

1. Remove the leaf net that has stopped leaves blowing into the pond during the winter.
2. Check pumps and electrics. Even very well-sealed weatherproof connections can be affected by a build-up of humidity from damp air.
3. Marginal plants: cut back any dead growth from the previous year that has not been dealt with already. Overgrown aquatic plants can be divided and replanted. This ought not to be done too early in northern and exposed areas as the old growth provides some cover for emerging growth and also to the fish. Oxygenators can be cut back once full growth has started. It is best to do a little bit at a time regularly rather than having to do a massive cut back that will give algae an opportunity to over-populate.
4. Fish feeding: build up slowly to daily feeding to ensure the fish are in peak condition for breeding. Feed wheatgerm-rich, low-protein varieties of food sparingly when temperatures are below 10°C (50°F) and above 7°C (45°F). Do not feed at all if temperatures are below 7°C. Even if the fish take food, it may not be digested and will only cause problems as it rots in their stomachs or guts. Fish food manufacturers are making improvements to their products all the time so, if in doubt about the most appropriate fish food for the time of year, consult a well-informed supplier. Once temperatures stabilise at above 15°C (60°F), you can feed high-protein food.
5. Clean out fountains and waterfalls.
6. If the pond is really dirty, clean out before the frogs spawn in mid-March to April.

Rather you than me. Brrr! October would be a better time if the cleaning can wait. The fish will be more able to take the stress by then.

Many fish keepers drain off between one half and one third of the pool water, replacing it with fresh water that has been conditioned with a proprietary pool conditioner or dechlorinator. This is particularly important if the pool water has had to be treated with medications or salt during the winter. They then add a dose of tonic or vitamins to help the fish after the weakening trials and tribulations of the winter by building up the protective mucous layer that is the fishes' only barrier to disease and many parasites.

Summer: June – September

1.   Evaporation may cause water levels to drop. Replenish the pond periodically with a hose, as sunlight on any liner material apart from concrete makes it deteriorate. Dropping the water in from a height helps to disperse some of the chlorine from tap water. Add a dechlorinator, particularly if evaporation occurs regularly.
2.   Net out thread algae. If green water is persistent, think about getting a filter. Either way, trouble-shoot it.
3.   Some early flowering plants, for example, the Calthas or Marsh Marigolds, may need cutting back to encourage a second flush of flower.
4.   As water temperatures rise above 15°C (60°F), feed the fish on high-protein foods and watch out for disease.
5.   New fish acclimatise easily as long as there is enough room for them.
6.   If you have a biological filter, leave it running all the time. The aerobic bacteria that build up in it, consuming the organic waste in the filter and transforming the ammonia and nitrites into relatively harmless nitrates, depend upon oxygen to survive. This is brought to them by a constant flow of water pumped through the filter. Keep the pre-filters to the pump clean.
7.   Beware of filter delicacy – it is working hard and cannot be cleaned too thoroughly, or you clean away the valuable aerobic bacteria that are working for you. Make sure you clean the filter with pond water or, at least, water without chlorine in it.
8.   If you have a fountain or waterfall, you might find it advisable to keep a hose pipe running into the pool, particularly on warm, sultry nights. See *Why in the Biological do I need a Filter?* (page 20) and *The Perfect Pond Detective Book 2: Trouble shooting filters.* This helps to replenish the oxygen supply in the water which will be very much needed because:
(a) at night the oxygenating plants cease to give out oxygen;
(b) as the water warms in the summer, it is less able to hold oxygen;
(c) the stillness of the air means that less oxygen is available at the surface of the pool;
(d) the metabolism of the fish increases immensely, adding ammonia to the water; this added ammonia increases the stress factor for the fish and causes them to secrete even more ammonia. This ammonia can only be broken down by the aerobic bacteria which, even if you have not got a filter, are still in the bottom of the pond digesting and breaking down organic matter and ammonia. They need oxygen to survive and they use it all the time;
(e) algae may take advantage of the conditions and, in a bloom of over-population and death, add further loading to the nitrogen cycle in the pool.

Winter: October to March

Leave rubbish and detritus to drain on the side for 24 hours. Any stranded pool life can wriggle its way back into the pool.

Autumn and Winter: October – March

1. Remove fallen leaves and dead foliage. Cover the pool and stream with a net. Take out lighting.
2. Dredge out any debris liable to rot in the pool. Serious fish keepers suggest that a partial water change of about one quarter might be in order, especially if there has been a drought. The theory is that a considerable concentration of dissolved solids will remain because of evaporation. Treat the fresh tap water with conditioner.

   If you are going to clean out the pool, then early October is the time to do it. You will remember which plants are which. The fish are fat and healthy, and should be capable

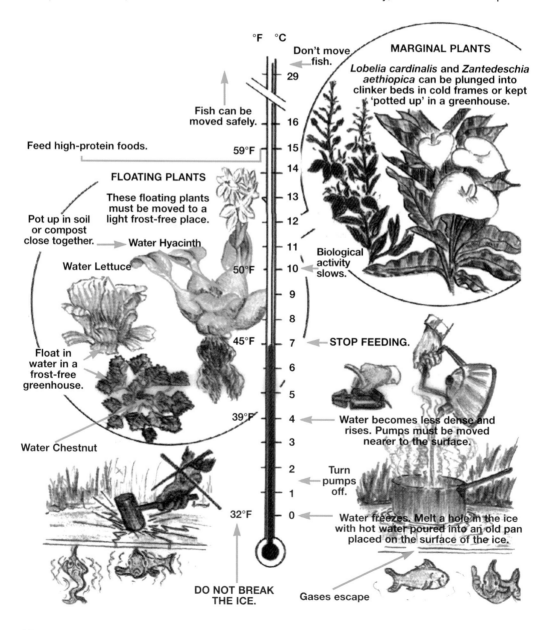

°F   °C

Don't move fish.

MARGINAL PLANTS

29

Lobelia cardinalis and *Zantedeschia aethiopica* can be plunged into clinker beds in cold frames or kept 'potted up' in a greenhouse.

Fish can be moved safely.   16

Feed high-protein foods.   59°F   15

14

FLOATING PLANTS

13

These floating plants must be moved to a light frost-free place.

Pot up in soil or compost close together. → Water Hyacinth   12

11

Water Lettuce   50°F   10   Biological activity slows.

9

8

Float in water in a frost-free greenhouse.   45°F   7   ← STOP FEEDING.

6

5

Water Chestnut   39°F   4   ← Water becomes less dense and rises. Pumps must be moved nearer to the surface.

3

2   Turn pumps off.

1

32°F   0   ← Water freezes. Melt a hole in the ice with hot water poured into an old pan placed on the surface of the ice.

DO NOT BREAK THE ICE.

Gases escape

of handling the trauma of the clean out. So will you, because the water is still fairly warm. Also, most of the hibernating frogs and toads will take the disturbance in their stride.

Once again, remember to 'condition' the fresh tap water you use to refill the pool.

3. Plants: remove tender aquatics from the pond. Floating plants that need winter protection include Water Hyacinths *(Eichornia crassipes)*. These can be potted-up close together in soil or compost. Water them in and store them in a light, frost-free place until late spring.

The Water Chestnut *(Trapa natans)*, the Chinese Water Chestnut *(Trapa bicornis)* and Water Lettuce *(Pistia stratiotes)* need to be floated in water in a frost-free greenhouse.

Of the marginal plants commonly found in retail outlets, *Lobelia fulgens* and *Zantedeschia aetheopica* are best either to 25cm (9in) below the water level, or brought into a frost-free greenhouse, or covered with ashes in a cold frame. *Zantedeschia aethiopica* 'Crowborough' is slightly more hardy and can be left in the pool.

Various marginal plants usually sold as tropicals very often find their way out into a colder environment. As winter sets in, the *Cyperus alternifolius* (Umbrella plant), *Cyperus papyrus* and the aquatic *Canna* hybrids must go indoors on to a sunny windowsill or into a heated greenhouse.

4. Pumps: surface pumps need protection and draining. Check submersible pumps for build-up of lime or silt on fins and bearing faces.

As the temperature of the water in the pool drops to around 4°C (39°F), instead of the warmer, less-dense water being at the surface, as in summer, the density of the water changes and the water that is closest to freezing becomes the least dense and floats to the top. The bottom stays at a fairly steady temperature under a blanket of colder water that may freeze.

If you wish to run a submersible pump, for example, for a biological filter, as it gets colder reduce its flow and bring it closer to the surface so that only the top 22–30cm (9–12in) of water in the pool are circulated. The depths of the pool will remain an even temperature by being left undisturbed.

5. Fish: Stop feeding the fish when the temperature drops below 7°C (45°F). They hibernate below 5°C (41°F). Between 7°C and 10°C (45–50°F), only feed very low protein foods two or three times a week and always remove uneaten food. If in doubt, **don't feed.**

6. Float a ball or a piece of wood in the pool or install a pool heater. This will maintain a hole in the ice that prevents the build-up of pressure on the sides of the pool and more effectively allows the escape of the toxic gases that build up under the surface of the ice.

Do not break the ice, it can stun the fish. Melt a hole with hot water. Sweep any snow away so that the oxygenators get some light.

7. Look out for herons, especially on still, foggy mornings.

8. Keep the pond topped up. If the water table in the surrounding soil rises above the water level in the pool, then the pool liner might lift and topple the baskets or, if it is a rigid liner, the pond might pop right out of the ground.

Why in the Biological do I need a Filter?

(See also *Cures for Green Water, Algae and Blanket Weed*, page 27.)

You might feel that you need a filter because your water is so green that you never see the fish. That might be your only reason. But it is *not* the reason you need the filter. The filter might enable you to see the fish, albeit for a short time, but you will not really have cured the cause of that green water. You have treated the 'headache', but not the cause of the 'headache'.

The green water is caused by millions of single-celled plants called algae that thrive in sunlight and feed off the excess nutrients in the pond water.

In a pond or pool, we want to establish what is described as the nitrogen cycle. All the organic matter in a pond (dead animals, bits of plant material and excrement), gets broken down by bacteria into chemicals that are actually of some benefit to the pond environment. These are mainly taken up as nutrition by the plants (including the algae if they get a look-in).

The high protein from the fish food, if it is allowed to rot on the bottom of the pool, together with the natural metabolism of fish, particularly Koi, and the excrement of fish, produce high concentrations of ammonia[1] (NH_3). This is highly toxic to fish and is usually broken down by nitrosomona bacteria on the bottom of the pond to nitrites[2] (NO_2) and then further by nitrobacteria to nitrates[3] (NO_3) – plant fertiliser. These bacteria need oxygen to survive and, indeed, the chemical process involves the linking-up of the nitrogen atoms in the ammonia with more and more oxygen.

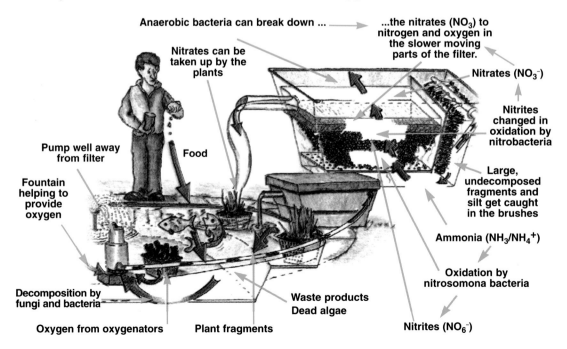

Anaerobic bacteria can break down ... → ...the nitrates (NO_3) to nitrogen and oxygen in the slower moving parts of the filter.

Nitrates can be taken up by the plants

Nitrates (NO_3^-)

Nitrites changed in oxidation by nitrobacteria

Pump well away from filter

Food

Large, undecomposed fragments and silt get caught in the brushes

Fountain helping to provide oxygen

Ammonia (NH_3/NH_4^+)

Oxidation by nitrosomona bacteria

Decomposition by fungi and bacteria

Waste products Dead algae

Oxygen from oxygenators

Plant fragments

Nitrites (NO_6^-)

Breaking down the organic matter.

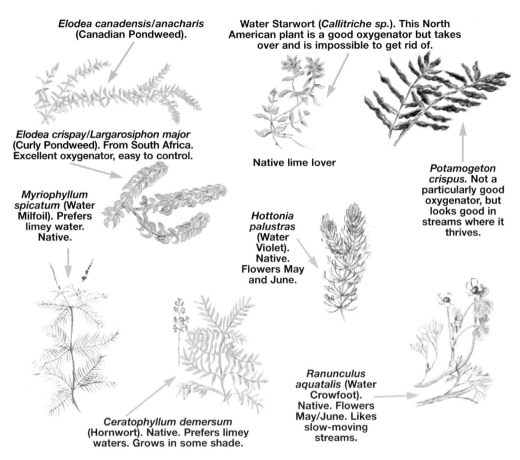

Elodea canadensis/anacharis (Canadian Pondweed).

Water Starwort (*Callitriche sp.*). This North American plant is a good oxygenator but takes over and is impossible to get rid of.

Elodea crispay/Largarosiphon major (Curly Pondweed). From South Africa. Excellent oxygenator, easy to control.

Native lime lover

Potamogeton crispus. Not a particularly good oxygenator, but looks good in streams where it thrives.

Myriophyllum spicatum (Water Milfoil). Prefers limey water. Native.

Hottonia palustras (Water Violet). Native. Flowers May and June.

Ceratophyllum demersum (Hornwort). Native. Prefers limey waters. Grows in some shade.

Ranunculus aquatalis (Water Crowfoot). Native. Flowers May/June. Likes slow-moving streams.

Oxygenating plants.

If the pond is highly stocked with fish, not only are the resources of oxygen under pressure from the respiration demands of the fish, but the chemical process of breaking down the waste is creating oxygen demand. The trouble is that if the fish themselves are under stress from the high level of toxins in the water, then their metabolism increases and they produce more ammonia directly from the gills. We therefore get a 'snowball effect' of pollutants.

The oxygenators in a pool are essential ingredients in the nitrogen cycle, using up the plant nutrients before the algae benefit from them and returning oxygen to the water. But the oxygen will not stay around long enough to be appreciated if there is too much ammonia about. Also, if your passion is for Koi, then the life expectancy of any oxygenators growing in the pool is pretty limited anyway, because the fish will gobble them up as they do virtually everything they can get in their mouths.

Therefore, in all the gradations from a pool being slightly overstocked to one of a monstrous environment where even the toughest water weed doesn't get a look in, it is probably good insurance (particularly in hedging against the extremes of the climate) to take what would commonly be happening in the bottom of the pool and put it on the side of the pool out of harm's way and under your control. This is the sort of filter we are talking about – an external or poolside biological filter. In order to be effective, it **must** run 24 hours a day; the constantly-fresh supply of oxygenated water is what keeps the

Rules and parameters for biological filter efficiency.

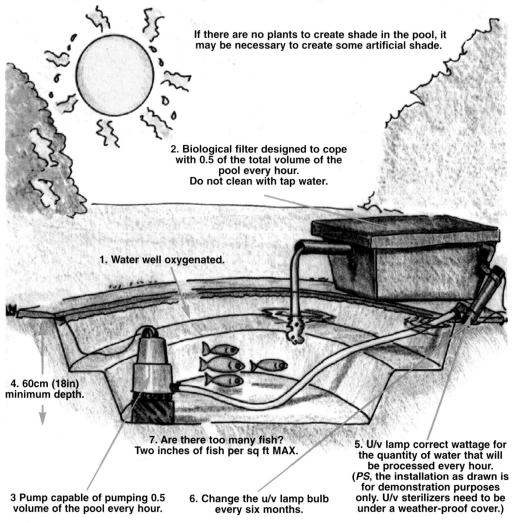

If there are no plants to create shade in the pool, it may be necessary to create some artificial shade.

2. Biological filter designed to cope with 0.5 of the total volume of the pool every hour. Do not clean with tap water.

1. Water well oxygenated.

4. 60cm (18in) minimum depth.

7. Are there too many fish? Two inches of fish per sq ft MAX.

3 Pump capable of pumping 0.5 volume of the pool every hour.

6. Change the u/v lamp bulb every six months.

5. U/v lamp correct wattage for the quantity of water that will be processed every hour. (*PS*, the installation as drawn is for demonstration purposes only. U/v sterilizers need to be under a weather-proof cover.)

filter's bacteria thriving. If they are deprived of this for even a couple of hours then they will start to die and the filter loses effectiveness.

What this filter also does is to remove algae from the pond water as it passes through, trapping it in the medium, allowing it to die and be digested by the bacteria population. This avoids any excess loading on the balance of the pond from the dead and decomposing algae. This process is doubly effective in conjunction with an ultra-violet (u/v) clarifier which 'zaps' the algae before it enters the filter box.

Before you get a filter you must examine your pool environment and assess whether:
- it is suitable to be equipped with a filter. There are different solutions to different problems in different pond environments. For instance, it would be silly to try to use a filter on a conservation/natural pond where the very definition of that type of pond dictates the encouragement of the ecological and self-contained cycle within the

pond without any intervention (particularly technological). Besides this, as many of these pools have soil bottoms, apart from containing all the necessary bacteria, the soil would soon clog up the pump and filter system.

- there may be seemingly unrelated problems which, if dealt with, might cure the problem with algae.
- there might be something else on the aquatic centre shelves that is more suitable for you. The reason why there are so many of these products and chemicals for treating fish and water is that whatever works for one person and their pond does not necessarily work for another. Each environment, the stocking levels, and the person managing the pond are all different. The water may be more acid or alkaline in one pool than the next. It might be because of water supply, soil run off, stone or cement surrounds, plant stocks or a host of other reasons. Because of all these, I recommend that before you are tempted to purchase any chemicals or buy a filter ponder, reflect and deduce exactly what is wrong and how it might otherwise be dealt with. Patience and compromise may be more expedient than the sledge hammer approach.

Rules and Parameters

For every pond there is a specific size of filter that needs a specific size of pump to recycle the water through it. Some manufacturers, using more sophisticated filter media and with ancillary accoutrements and 'add-ons' such as ultra-violet lamps and magnets, have reduced the size theoretically necessary to keep ponds of specific volumes clear, but they stick to some of the old rules for pond filtration.

- The pond must be at least 0.5m (18in) deep.
- The filter itself must be capable of processing half the volume of the pool every hour of the day and night.
- Therefore there must be a pump that is capable of delivering this.
- The water must be well oxygenated by waterfall, fountain or plants.

Over-specification is better than under-specification within reason. If the filter is churning over more than the **total** volume of the pool every hour, the resulting commotion underwater can only be to the detriment of the fish.

Example
A 500-gallon pond needs a filter that is related to that gallonage, together with a pump that can deliver 250 gallons to the height at which the filter is sitting. Situate the pump on the opposite side of the pond to the filter inlet for efficiency.

It used to be necessary to have a filter surface area that was one-third of the pool surface area. Modern manufacturers with compact multi-stage units claim otherwise. But it is useful to bear this in mind, since a manufacturer's claim to guaranteeing water *clarity* does not guarantee the *quality* of that water. After all, water containing ammonia and nitrites can still be quite clear.

Problems in a filter are often the result of the original reason for needing a filter rearing its ugly head again. On the other hand, they might not be. A process of elimination must be followed.

Pollution leading to stress in fish

1 Bonfires, car exhaust and fag ends.
2 Overhead flying aircraft.
3 Trees: yew, elder, oak or willow.
4 Fresh, untreated tap water.
5 Overfeeding – the most common pollutant.
6 Unsuitable food: old sandwiches.
7 Paint solvents, wood stains and wood preservatives.
8 Lime leaching in from concrete (concrete ponds) or cement from under slabs.
9 Slabs cambered in the wrong direction allowing ingress of nitrates or weedkillers in solution of rain.
10 Lime leaching in from limestone edging.
11 Flymos and rotary mowers blow in debris and lawn fertilizer.
12 Metal poisoning from new copper fittings and galvanising.

Environmental factors leading to stress which in turn causes water problems

A Predators: herons and cats. Disturbance by dogs and clumsiness with the net.

B Too many fish.

C Koi carp in the pool without the benefit of filter technology.

D Koi carp grazing planting baskets.

E Not enough oxygenators and plants that provide pool cover in conditions of full sun.

F Large, too-shallow areas create heat, generating ideal conditions for algae.

Water Chemistry

Most experts in fish keeping propound that the susceptibility of fish to all pests and diseases is directly related to the quality of their environment – the water they live in. Therefore, when looking for a permanent cure to any fish ailments, the answer lies in intelligent water management. If you do not have a water testing kit, your problems with water chemistry might be manifested in problems with algae (green water), fish health problems or fish behaviour problems.

Poor Water Quality

Poor water quality can be linked to one or several causes:

1. Lack of oxygen, especially in green water.
2. Overstocking. You should have only 2in of fish per square foot of surface area.
3. Over feeding the fish, especially in winter. Do not feed when the temperature is below 10°C (50°F).
4. Decaying fish food or a build-up of decaying plant matter. Net off all excess food after feeding time. Only feed what the fish can eat in 5–10 minutes.
5. Stress caused by anything in this list. Stress increases a fish's metabolism, which in turn pollutes its environment, causing further stress.
6. Pollution can come in a variety of forms:
   (a) Fertilisers and weed killers leaching in or drifting in on spray.
   (b) Lime or cement chemicals leaching in from fresh ornaments, from stone edging or from under newly-laid paving edging.
   (c) Chemical treatments and preservatives and solvents used on woodwork for jetties or decking.
   (d) Metal poisoning from, for example, copper fittings used in the plumbing of pumps, or galvanised mesh, or money.
   (e) Trees and other plant life in the vicinity, especially oak, elder, yew and willow.
   (f) Bonfires, traffic, overhead aircraft.

Any of these factors causes stress to the fish, so the fishes' metabolism increases and they produce excess ammonia from their gills. In a confined environment the ammonia is highly toxic and in its turn causes the fish even more stress. A downward spiral therefore quickly develops in a small pool. This fact is repeated several times in this book, if only to emphasise the importance of the quality of the environment on the health of the fish. Prevention is better than cure, so it is vital to start on the right footing (see Chapter 2).

   (g) The filter itself can be the polluting agent. If a toxic-producing colony of bacteria has become established through irregular use or lack of management of the filter, then the cause of the stress does not register on any water-testing equipment. If this is suspected after a water test, clean out the filter and start again with a fresh medium.

Adding Fish Whilst Maintaining Water Quality

1. Make sure the pond is stocked with the relevant quantities of plants. Try to wait 3–4

weeks so that the plants become established before adding any fish (see Chapter 2 *Avoiding Problems from the Start*, and *Establishing your Pond* and *Stocking Levels,* see pages 7 and 8).

2   Introduce the fish in late spring. Do not get too many at once. Small fish will be more prone to problems because of their relative frailty. Larger fish take longer to settle in a new environment.

3.   Do not move the fish at very high or very low temperatures: 10°C (50°F) is too low, 32°C (90°F) is too high.

4.   When buying fish, take your time. Choose healthy stock. If a number of fish in the retailer's tank look unwell, then better not buy any. Avoid bargains and end-of-season sales.

5.   Expect a pond that has been filled with fresh tap water to go through a green phase, at least until a large body of oxygenating weed is established and some plants are covering and shading the surface. Avoid using algicides on new ponds. A chemical additive for 'conditioning' or 'aging' fresh tap water may help you to avoid the green stage.

6.   After this, avoid all the potential causes of water problems and check that none has arisen. This may be easier said than done since, for instance, the causes of green water or a bloom of algae can be a subtle blend of innumerable causes which by themselves may not have any significant effect.

Cures for Green Water, Algae and Blanket Weed (Spirogyra)

All water contains algae and in itself and, under normal conditions, this is not necessarily a problem. It may be a symptom of any of the above effects and therefore the cause or causes are the problem. To restrict the growth of algae:

1.   Increase the oxygen level of the pond. Aerate either mechanically by moving the water through stream or fountain, or by plants. Increase the numbers of oxygenators. These will compete with the algae for the same nutritional minerals in the environment. They will also provide oxygen for the bacteria in the bottom of the pool or filter and thus give a welcome boost to the life/nitrogen cycle of the pond.

2.   Floating plants are a quick and effective addition to the pool because they provide shade and use up the plant nutrients in the pool that might otherwise be capitalised on by the algae. Water Hyacinth *(Eichornia crassipes)* works particularly well, although is not welcomed in the warmer parts of the United States because it is so prolific.

3.   For the longer term, lilies provide shade and use up any nitrates that may be in the water. In fact, all other plants are on your side. The marginal plants help to use up the nitrates that even the most efficient biological filter cannot deal with.

4.   Remove excess fish. Avoid having more than 2in of fish per square foot of surface area.

5.   Only feed the fish as much they can eat in five minutes. Floating fish food is suitable for most fish and any excess can be netted off.

6.   Any shallows and backwaters can become 'algae factories'. Try to get some higher plants established in these areas. What is the point in having a beach effect if it is always covered in blanket weed?

7.   If you haven't already got a biological filter, then consider obtaining one. You may only be buying time if there is something else inherently wrong with your pool balance. Also remember that, if the problem is caused by persistent pollution, a filter will not be a 'cure' as such. Once you have a filter you are committed to running it all day and every day, apart from in the very frozen depths of winter. If you have a filter:

   (a) is it big enough, and is the pump feeding the pool water turning over the total volume of the pond every two hours; and

   (b) is the pump well away from the filter unit so that all the water in the pond circulates through the filter?

8.   If you haven't already got a u/v steriliser, then consider getting one. But you will need some sort of filtration system as well. It is essential that the steriliser treats the water going **into** the filter.

   Keep the quartz sleeve clean. A further aid is a magnet that lies in line before the u/v lamp and helps to prevent hard water from building up deposits on the inside of the unit. It also discourages the build-up of the long strings of cell growth in blanket weed.

9.   If you have a large Koi set-up that does not have the benefit of plants to do the work in the final stage of the nitrogen cycle, then you must consider adding an anaerobic stage to your filtration. An extension to the filter that uses aerobic bacteria to digest basic organic material passes water much more slowly through a medium in which a colony of anaerobic bacteria is established. These bacteria work much more slowly and do not need oxygen to survive. They are capable of breaking down the nitrates into their basic oxygen and nitrogen building blocks. Alternatively, see *Reed bed system*, page 29.

10. If you do not want to become dependent on technology, try barley straw. It works for most people. However, you need plenty of oxygen as well.

Recipe
5g of barley straw per 1000 litres (220 gal) of water
pack into open-meshed sacks
keep straw on the surface and exposed to sunlight
circulate water to distribute effect
ensure the water is well oxygenated
allow one full month for it to take effect
replenish every six months

The retailers and manufacturers of barley straw products assure me that, although it will not eradicate huge massed quantities of blanket weed, if customers do their best to remove the majority of that which plagues them, then the chemistry will begin to work in their favour.

11. For 'natural' pools, try products such as 'Aquaplankton' which come as a powder that stimulates the bacterial growth in the bottom of the pond. The pond needs to be well-oxygenated for the products to work effectively.

12. If you don't have fish, introduce daphnia. These tiny creatures (which fish love to eat) consume algae. If algae flourishes, then so do they – natural control.

13. It is also important to shift down the pH of the water, particularly for the control of blanket weed. Blanket weed only develops at pH above 7. When the pH rises, the toxic effect of any ammonia in the water rises. Therefore, stress from any lime in the water is made that much more unbearable to the fish with their own ammonia excretions. The pH

of the pond can be effectively reduced with chemicals or a 'peat pellet teabag'. The latter method is rapidly losing favour in the light of current opinion that we should avoid using non-renewable resources.

14. Many people believe that green water is dirty water, and the truth may be that the situation has got well beyond the help of any filtration or chemical inoculation. Quite simply, the pool needs a good clean.

Remember that if you do go for the complete clean-out option, you will have to wait for your new pond water to go through an 'aging' process, which generally means it will turn green, although only temporarily. Treating fresh tap water with a conditioner can sometimes avoid this phase. It helps to run the water in from a height.

Other Considerations
Reed bed system: Create a cascade of containers. Three is generally enough, one above the other, all containing gravel in which fast-growing marginal plants are planted. Water is pumped up from the pond, flows in at the top of the top container, flows from one container to another and eventually back into the pond after having passed through the root systems of the plants.

This system not only clarifies the water but rids it of masses of toxins and pollutants that most other filter systems don't come anywhere near to removing. Norfolk reed and Watercresses are particularly good. In my experience, Villarsia (*Nymphoides peltata*) works well too. (See also *Nitrates* on page 34, and the illustration on page 33.)

Other Visible Water Problems
Scum or oil: Drag underlay or cardboard across the pond. This is slow but sure. Larger pools can be dealt with by a boom created from a floating sausage of straw, linen, socks or wool. In an emergency, 'necessity is the mother of invention'.

Red water: Common in bird baths and small bodies of water, this is a red algae (*Rhodophyceae class*), perhaps *Batrachospermum*. In my experience, this algae seems to be a pioneer and merely heralds the arrival of the more proliferate green algae.

Brown water: This is usually a sign of mud-stirring fish activity or turbulence. Rain can also batter particles into the pool or stream. Koi carp digging around in lily baskets are the bane of many water gardeners' lives. To cure brown water:
- put heavy pebbles on the surface of the baskets;
- surround the plant with a 'Netlon' tube to protect the plant to the surface;
- make a fish-free zone in the pond reserved exclusively for plants.
Alternatively, get rid of the tench and the Koi.

Clear brown water, like tea, can be the result of the leaching of minerals from the surrounding rocks and soil or peat bogs. Tannins can also diffuse out of leaves such as oak to produce a similar staining effect.

Black water: If you push a stick into a pond containing water like this, bubbles rise to the surface. This is due to the decay of organic matter. The bacteria involved in this process are not the desirable ones and are producing poisonous gas and toxins. Nearby trees will be shedding their leaves into the water and it is likely that some of them contain toxins as well.

The organic matter in the bottom must be removed as soon as possible. Do not disturb it too much as it will poison the water even more. There is probably little enough oxygen in there anyway, so a partial water change will help as an emergency measure until it is feasible to do a total clean out.

Try to net the pond before the leaf fall in autumn to prevent this becoming a perennial problem.

Milky water: It is highly likely that there is a dead fish or animal decomposing in the pond. Get it out and change the water.

The perfect pond detective needs to be armed with:

Information
gallonage of pool

magnifying glass

water test kit

net

Perfect Pond Detective Book

thermometer

Unseen Water Problems

There is a school of thought that says a little bit of knowledge in this department can be a bad thing; that if you start off with all the right ingredients and keep within the prescribed parameters then a natural biological balance will evolve eventually. The less you tamper and test, pry and manipulate, the more the environmental system will be able to look after itself.

This is all very well, until the pond begins to realise its ambition to become a 'boggy place'.

The first signs that there is a problem with the water will be shown by the behaviour of the fish. They may be sluggish, be gasping at the surface, or exhibiting peculiar behaviour such as 'flashing' or rubbing themselves on the sides of the pool.

If the problem seems to be affecting most or all of the fish then it is likely to be a water problem or an indirect result of poor water quality. It may be that the poor water quality is caused by the fish. They may be so overcrowded that they are causing themselves stress. The water will be tainted by their excretions anyway but, once a fish is in a stressful environment, the excretions become that much more toxic and therefore that much more stressful. This is particularly so with Koi carp, which excrete ammonia from their gills. Ironically, ammonia is a poison to which they are extremely sensitive. Very quickly the resilient film that coats the fish and acts as a barrier to all the bacteria, fungi and some of the parasites loses its effectiveness.

Signs of poor water quality as manifested by fish in their behaviour are:
- *gasping at the surface:* ammonia, nitrite or pH levels are very high; lack of oxygen;
- *flashing or wriggling:* very high pH; chlorine in tap water;
- *lethargy and poor colour:* metal poisoning, especially copper from coins thrown into the pool.

Many of these symptoms can indicate diseases or parasites, so it is essential that a thorough analysis of the water is carried out in order to get a complete picture of the health of the fish. Having said this, poor water quality induces a greater propensity to disease and susceptibility to parasites.

Emergency Treatment
It may be necessary to do something about the situation even before analysing the water.
1. Run a hose pipe into the pond from a height and let it gently overflow.
2. The action of the above might help to oxygenate the pond, but supplement this by turning on a fountain or waterfall. An air pump or venturi system would be even better. Oxygenating water actually has the effect of chasing out the carbon dioxide dissolved in water. This will be present in the form of carbonic acid, therefore oxygenation will have the effect of raising the pH of the water.
3. Analyse the water, particularly the pH, and proceed with the diagnosis.
4. A tonic dosage of salt (300g per 100l) will reduce the effects of ammonia and help the fish to restore their mucous membrane.

pH

The pH of water is a measurement of the concentration of ions in a solution (hydrogen ions). This determines whether the water is acid, neutral or alkaline. This is measured on a scale of 1 (very acid) to 14 (very alkaline), pH 7 being neutral. The scale is logarithmic and therefore the increase of pH 1 is effectively an increase to the power of 10. It follows that the increase in pH between 8 and 9 is vastly different in proportion to that between 7 and 8.

What Affects pH?
Respiration of fish: Fish taking in oxygen release carbon dioxide (CO_2). This dissolves in water to produce carbonic acid.

Effect: More acid.
Cure: Increase the oxygen level using aerator, fountain, fresh water.

Respiration of plants: All plants use carbon dioxide (CO_2) during photosynthesis during which the plants manufacture their food using sunlight. Nitrates are also used up in the growth process.
Effect: Raises pH; more alkaline.

Biological filtration:
(a) Where a condition exists where aerobic bacteria are breaking down toxic substances into less harmful ones; ammonia (NH_3) is broken down into nitrites (NO_2^{-1}) and then down to nitrates (NO_3^{-1}). This is described as 'nitrification'.
Effect: More acid; the nitrate ions and the hydrogen released form nitric acid.

(b) There may be a stage in the filter system in which anaerobic activity occurs, where nitrates might be broken down into nitrogen and oxygen. This activity, called denitrification, is generally only found in the more sophisticated filter systems. Usually it is performed by the plants or bacteria in the muddy depths of the pond.
Effect: Raises pH.

Fresh tap water: Fresh tap water contains innumerable dissolved substances which depend, to an extent, on which rocks it flowed over in nature and what seeped into it from land as it passed through the countryside. The main bulk of the compounds that might be found in tap water contribute to its hardness. These are mainly magnesium and calcium salts and have a direct effect on the alkalinity (pH) of the water.
Effect: Raises pH.
Cure: Condition the water with a proprietary pool conditioner.

Untreated cement products such as edging stones, cement pointing, fresh concrete ornaments leach calcium carbonate into the water.
Effect: Raises pH.
Cure: Treat exposed cement with Silglaze. 'Weather' any limestone product as rapidly as possible.

Oxygen

Oxygen is as essential to fish as it is to humans. The level of oxygen that it is possible to maintain in water drops radically as the temperature of the water rises. At night, when the oxygenating plants cannot release oxygen as a by-product of photosynthesis but produce carbon dioxide instead, it becomes critical that the eco-system established in your pond does not come under any further pressures. If, for instance, there is a great deal of bacterial activity in the bottom of the pond for the breakdown of waste and organic matter, this will further deplete the limited resource of oxygen. The oxygen content will be at its lowest between 6 and 7am so test the water then. It needs to be 1mg/1l.

Lack of Oxygen
Effects: Fish gasping at the surface especially on a hot, humid, overcast evening.
Emergency treatment: Oxygenate with an air pump, venturi, fountain, waterfall or, if necessary, a hose with force from a height.

Emergency treatment for lack of oxygen.

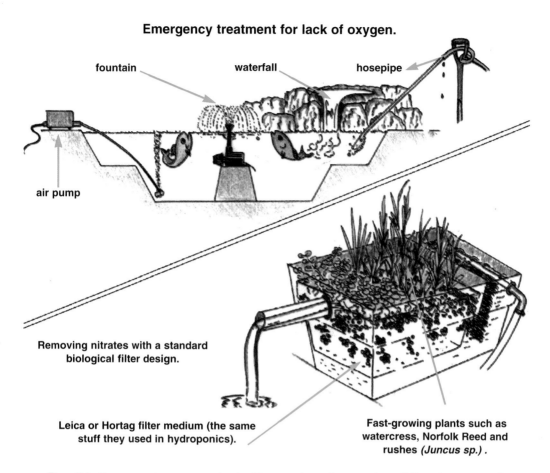

fountain   waterfall   hosepipe

air pump

Removing nitrates with a standard
biological filter design.

Leica or Hortag filter medium (the same
stuff they used in hydroponics).

Fast-growing plants such as
watercress, Norfolk Reed and
rushes *(Juncus sp.)* .

Possibly there are too many plants; if so, reduce the number. If the plants are algae, carry out a partial water change with conditioner, then treat as for nitrates with a view to cleaning out.

Cure: Increase oxygen on a permanent basis, ie, increase oxygenating plants.

Too Much Oxygen

Effects: Fish get bubbles in their blood and fins. It has the same effect as the 'bends' suffered by divers. The fish become bloated and look as though they are suffering from dropsy.

Emergency treatment: Gently run in fresh water from a hose pipe.

Cure: Reduce oxygenation – remove some of the weed.

Chemical Compounds

These invisible nitrogenous compounds are present in the water as a result of the normal nitrogen cycle of the pond or pool. They should be broken down quickly by the bacteria in the bottom of the pool or in the filter. For the nitrogen cycle to function efficiently, an adequate amount of oxygen needs to be available in the water for the bacteria to begin to process the toxic chemicals. If, as a result of some imbalance or stress in the environment, ammonia or nitrites build up, then the fish will soon die.

Ammonia

Ammonia in minute proportions is toxic to fish. It is present in fish excreta and is even exuded from the gills of Koi carp. This release increases as the fish become unhappy with their environment, which in turn increases their discomfort. A spiral of deterioration is created.

Effect: Even at a dilution of 0.25mg/l, the toxicity of ammonia can become critical. Even a fraction of this concentration increases susceptibility to diseases and irritates the gills of sensitive fish. A rise in pH makes matters worse and increases the ammonia's toxicity.

Emergency treatment:
(a) Partial water change of up to one third of the pool water volume. This may be necessary every day until the problem subsides.
(b) Pump in oxygen.
(c) Check that the filter, if present, is functioning adequately. It may be clogged up. Lacking in oxygen, it may be colonised by the wrong type of bacteria that could be making matters worse. Does it smell right? I hope you haven't just turned it on after leaving it standing stagnant and idle all winter, or having left it standing for even a day or two in the summer. (See Book 2, *Mechanical and Physical Problems*, *Filter Problems*, page 41.)
(d) Try to remove some of the sludge and detritus from the bottom of the pond, although this can make matters worse if it is not done carefully. There might be a case for a total clean out if the material cannot be effectively siphoned or vacuumed out.
(e) Adding salt at the rate of 30g/1l as a tonic reduces the toxicity of ammonia and nitrites. Avoid giving successive doses without a total clean out.
(f) If you have a biological filter, obviously it is not working yet. It may be too cold or may not have built up a colony of the necessary bacteria. Try adding a dose of filter culture from a successful working filter or a proprietary product such as 'Pond Start'.

Nitrites

Nitrites are the compounds formed in the first stage of the breakdown of ammonia to the relatively harmless nitrates. Nitrifying bacteria need a continuous supply of oxygen in order to complete this process. The nitrite concentration should not exceed 0.2mg nitrite nitrogen per litre of water.

Effects: The blood of the fish is contaminated and the haemoglobin is prevented from carrying oxygen around the body. The result is that the fish gasps for air at the surface of the water, breathing rapidly. Prolonged levels of low toxicity produce poor coloration, weak growth and a greater susceptibility to disease.

Emergency treatment: Treat as for ammonia above.

Nitrates

1.   These compounds are relatively much less toxic than nitrites and ammonia. At levels 50mg/l they begin to affect fish, especially fry. They retard growth and particularly hinder the development of fins. Coloration begins to be affected and the fish are more prone to disease. Koi are less susceptible and have been known to tolerate levels of up to 500mg/l.

Effects: Any level of nitrates above 12.5mg/l tend to promote the growth of algae. The nitrate concentration can, however, get worse in a pond with an efficient filter with few or no plants. It is further exacerbated by the use of a u/v sterilizer, over-crowding by fish and over-feeding. The filter is effectively killing the algae that would be utilising the nitrates and, in the course of processing filtered material from ammonia through to nitrites, it ends up feeding even more nitrates back into the pool.

2.   With even low levels of nitrates encouraging the growth of algae, the susceptibility to the scourge of blanket weed is by far the worst problem. Also with the higher levels of nitrates the threat of the blue-green algaes loom and these can become toxins that spell the death of all life in the pond.

Emergency treatment: (a) partial water change and (b) remove excessive detritus from the filter.

Cures: Try all of the suggestions below.

(a) Encourage healthy plant growth in the pond. Oxygenating weeds are the most effective.

(b) If this is not possible, then you must add an anaerobic stage to your filter system. Here denitrifying bacteria can break down the nitrates to nitrogen and oxygen. I have never had much success with this, and find it easier to work with plants. Even if necessity forces you to do this outside the pool, you can use the missing link in the nitrogen cycle to work in your favour. Grow plants, particularly fast-growing ones such as Watercress, in the filtration media to use up the nitrates in the water as it passes through. (See *Reed bed system*, page 29.)

(c) Ensure the pond is never overstocked with fish.

(d) Do not overfeed the fish, especially when the temperature of the water drops below 8°C (46°F).

(e) Does the pond need to be cleaned out?

Chlorine and Chloramine

Chlorine and chloramine (a more stable form of chlorine compound) are added to the water supplies by the water companies in compound form to keep the water we consume free from pests and diseases. Unfortunately, these chemicals and the free chlorine gas that remains in the water are highly toxic, especially to Koi.

Much of the gas can be dispelled by spraying the water into the pond at pressure. Any further chlorine will be expelled by further oxygenation. This may take anything from 7–10 days, during which we say that the water 'ages'.

This process can be speeded up with the use of a proprietary chemical, 'Pool Conditioner'. This will dissipate not only the chlorine but any other halogens. It will also help the heavy metals common in our water supplies to drop out harmlessly. The fish are further helped by a special protective colloid that mimics their natural secretions and so helps to protect them from their environment and reduce the effects of stress. This makes it doubly useful if you have to move the fish for any reason, and it is an essential additive for whenever you have to top up or do a partial water change.

General Fish Care

Well-nourished fish in a well-managed pool have strong natural resistance to potentially harmful organisms that constantly surround them. When feeding, remember that:
(a) by mid-April, fish can accept food every day;
(b) it is better to give a light meal morning and evening than to give one heavy feed;
(c) remove uneaten food after 10 minutes.

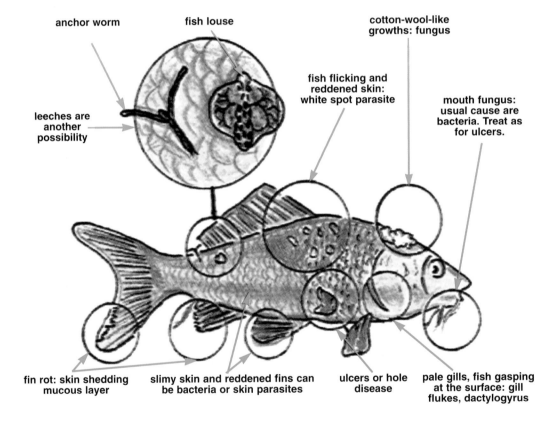

anchor worm

fish louse

cotton-wool-like growths: fungus

fish flicking and reddened skin: white spot parasite

mouth fungus: usual cause are bacteria. Treat as for ulcers.

leeches are another possibility

fin rot: skin shedding mucous layer

slimy skin and reddened fins can be bacteria or skin parasites

ulcers or hole disease

pale gills, fish gasping at the surface: gill flukes, dactylogyrus

Fish Problems

Most fish pathogens are found either on the fish or in the pool environment in small numbers. In good conditions, the fish's immune system is increased by the presence of pathogens, which act almost like a natural vaccination.

Where conditions in the pool are not ideal (low water quality combined with other stressful factors), the organisms that are normally kept at bay are given the opportunity to thrive. For instance, after a long winter with little opportunity to digest food at low temperatures, the fish are no longer resistant to parasitic, bacterial, fungal or viral activity which is revived at much lower temperatures than the fish's immune system. In fact, as

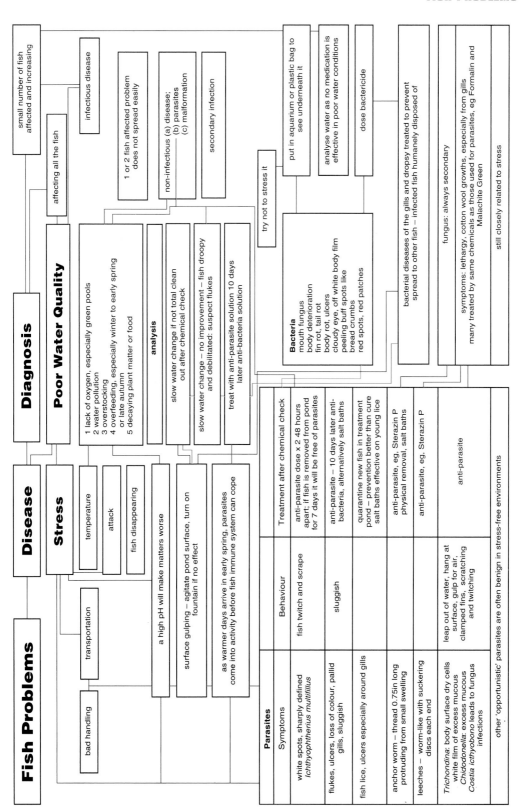

Fish Problems

Diagnosis

- small number of fish affected and increasing
- affecting all the fish → infectious disease
- 1 or 2 fish affected problem does not spread easily
- non-infectious (a) disease; (b) parasites; (c) malformation
- secondary infection

Disease · **Stress** · **Poor Water Quality**

Stress:
- bad handling
- transportation
- temperature
- attack
- fish disappearing

a high pH will make matters worse

surface gulping – agitate pond surface, turn on fountain if no effect

as warmer days arrive in early spring, parasites come into activity before fish immune system can cope

Poor Water Quality:
1. lack of oxygen, especially green pools
2. water pollution
3. overstocking
4. overfeeding, especially winter to early spring or late autumn
5. decaying plant matter or food

analysis
- slow water change if not total clean out after chemical check
- slow water change – no improvement – fish droopy and debilitated: suspect flukes
- treat with anti-parasite solution 10 days later anti-bacteria solution

try not to stress it

put in aquarium or plastic bag to see underneath it

analyse water as no medication is effective in poor water conditions

dose bactericide

Bacteria
- mouth fungus
- body deterioration
- fin rot, tail rot
- body rot, ulcers
- cloudy eye, off white body film
- peeling buff spots like bread crumbs
- red spots, red patches

bacterial diseases of the gills and dropsy treated to prevent spread to other fish – infected fish humanely disposed of

fungus: always secondary

symptoms: lethargy, cotton wool growths, especially from gills many treated by same chemicals as those used for parasites, eg Formalin and Malachite Green

still closely related to stress

Parasites		
Symptoms	Behaviour	Treatment after chemical check
white spots, sharply defined *Ichthyophtherius multifilius*	fish twitch and scrape	anti-parasite dose x 2 48 hours apart; if fish is removed from pond for 7 days it will be free of parasites
flukes, ulcers, loss of colour, pallid gills, sluggish	sluggish	anti-parasite – 10 days later anti-bacteria, alternatively salt baths
fish lice, ulcers especially around gills		quarantine new fish in treatment pond – prevention better than cure salt baths effective on young lice
anchor worm – thread 0.75in long protruding from small swelling		anti-parasite, eg, Sterazin P physical removal, salt baths
leeches – worm-like with suckering discs each end		anti-parasite, eg, Sterazin P
Trichondina: body surface dry cells white film of excess mucous *Chlodonella*: excess mucous *Costia icthyobono* leads to fungus infections	leap out of water, hang at surface, gulp for air, clamped fins, scratching and twitching	anti-parasite
other 'opportunistic' parasites are often benign in stress-free environments		

37

the temperatures of the fish world warm up, their immune system struggles to keep in control. Then when a sudden unexpected cold snap occurs, we might find a sudden spiral of pathogen population taking advantage of a faltering immune system. Koi in particular might suddenly succumb to septicaemia or ulcer disease.

Procedure

1. Identify and deal with the cause of distress.
    (a) Check water quality. If you cannot test it yourself, get a local aquatic centre to help.
    (b) Note when you first noticed the problem.
    (c) Is just one or are all the fish affected, and are the symptoms getting worse?
    (d) Make a note of the symptoms.
    These observations are essential in case you find it necessary to call in expert help or if the disease has occurred since the purchase and introduction of some new fish.
2. Improve water quality.
3. Diagnose and treat the disease. If an individual fish is diseased, this may mean removing it from its environment (ideally to an aquarium), particularly if other fish are breeding. This will also help to prevent harassment from other fish. You now have the opportunity to ensure that the patient receives high-quality food, little and often, and with no fat. Do not feed during treatment unless it is just a salt treatment.
    It will also be easier to treat the disease by swabs, dips or baths. You can control the fluid balance by giving a salt treatment of 3g/1l water. Removing the fish to an aquarium will cause it less stress all round than constantly removing it from the pond environment.

Treatment

General Points of Treatment
Many fish problems can be effectively treated with proprietary treatments from the shelves of most aquatic centres.
1. Read the instructions carefully.
2. Treating in a pond? Do not introduce fish to a recently-dosed pond and do not add new water during treatment.
3. Refrain from feeding prior to any treatment.
4. Dose correctly. If the patient is 'hospitalized' in a tank of measurable size, then it is easy to give the correct dosage. The effect can be seen and the chemical is not wasted. Hospitalization might be necessary if you propose to use organophosphate chemicals since these are poisonous to orfe and rudd and the dosage for other fish needs to be very accurate.
5. If you do treat the fish in a hospital tank or pond, aeration may be necessary to ensure a satisfactory level of oxygen, as many treatments reduce the oxygen level in water. Remembering that oxygen levels drop at night, this is doubly important because many medicines seem to be more effective if administered at night. Bear this in mind even for pond treatments.

Warning
1. Do not use any proprietary treatment containing formalin or potassium permanganate with any salt.

2. Some fish diseases can infect humans. Use rubber gloves or plastic bags when handling diseased fish and disinfect nets afterwards.

3. Handle poisonous chemicals with care. If they are poisonous to parasites or bacteria, they are liable to be poisonous at certain toxicities to fish and to you.

4. Some chemicals can affect the performance of your biological filter system.

Different Methods of Treatment

There are three main methods of treatment:

Dips: The fish is placed in a tank of very concentrated treatment solution for a very short time.

Baths: The fish is kept in perhaps a more dilute concentration of the chemical for a longer period of time, for example in a 3% salt solution tonic for 10 minutes unless the fish shows distress.

Swabs: Concentrated solution is applied by swab directly to the wound with the fish out of water. This can be stressful for the fish. (See *Procedure* above.)

Some of the more common fish problems are given below. It is not an exhaustive diagnostic summary, but it will serve as a guide for treatment in the majority of cases.

Diagnosis

The diagnosis of the cause of death can only be relevant if death has taken place within the last 20 minutes. After death, most of the outside parasites will have dispersed and the micro-organisms will have spread like wild-fire. This will undoubtedly result in a misleading conclusion. But, having said this, hopefully you will make a diagnosis before there is a body on your hands.

Behaviour is, therefore, the first indication that a fish is not well. It may be gulping for air at the surface, indicating lack of oxygen in the water or gill flukes or a bacterial infection of the gills. The fish may hide from other fish with its fins clamped in. This may be a bacterial infection or a parasitic infestation. Flitting, jumping and scraping against hard surfaces can be a reaction to parasites or simply skittishness at spawning time.

For many fish, spawning time can come when they are physically at quite a low ebb. The trials of a cool late spring may mean that many fish become very prone to infection, not having been able to build themselves up after a long hard winter. Therefore, keep an eye open for problems after any manifestations of fishy madness.

Fungal Diseases

Saprolegnia

Saprolegnia is usually secondary to other infections. It is not itself infectious.

Symptoms: Cottonwool growth on any part of the fish. Low temperatures allow it to attach when the fish's immune system is at its least effective, such as after spawning or after a long, hard winter.

Treatment: Check water, particularly the pH. Also check for physical damage. Give a proprietary treatment or a Malachite Green bath of 2mg/l for 30 minutes. Some experts would recommend gently swabbing away as much of the fungus as possible with a 10% solution of povidone iodine.

Branchyiomyces
This is a fungal disease that affects the gills of fish that stir up the bottom of the pool. It is not very common and can only be introduced to the pool by new fish.
Symptoms: The behavioural symptoms are very similar to those caused by many other diseases, and include lethargy, respiring heavily, not feeding and staying near the surface. The gills show cottonwool growths.
Treatment: Isolate and treat for fungus. It infects the whole system of the fish so quickly that treatment might come too late.

Bacteria
Bacteria such as aeromonas and pseudomonas are external bacteria always present in the environment, but they are opportunistic in their invasion of the body of the fish. This opportunity arises from possible physical damage caused by bad handling, fighting or fin nibbling. Stress from overcrowding or water quality is a major factor in this. Nitrites in the water can cause the fish to flick and rub themselves against solid objects. This may cause an injury that leaves the fish open to bacteria. In addition, parasites such as anchor worm, whitespot and fish louse can create a wound that can rapidly become infected by bacteria and develop into an ulcer.
Symptoms: Descriptive names of various types of bacterial infection are: mouth fungus (reddened lips, loose white tissue around the mouth); body deterioration; fin rot; tail rot; body rot; ulcers; cloudy eye. Symptoms are off white body film, peeling skin, buff spots like bread crumbs, red spots or patches.
Treatment: Treat the primary cause – improve water quality and reduce stress. Dose with a bactericide according to the instructions. Some bacteria can pass from fish to fish or from infected nets. Isolate the fish if the infection is bad and disinfect the net in a bactericide solution.

Sudden Death
With no real signs of the cause, unexplained death may be the result of sudden changes in water temperature, or the quality of the water producing stress that suppresses the immune system to the extent that the bacterial aeromonas and pseudomonas that normally populate the gills, skin and intestines of the fish get into the blood supply and poison it with septicaemia. This can also result in Haemorrhagic Septicaemia or ulcers.

Haemorrhagic Septicaemia
Symptoms: Streaks of red in the skin and fins. Fins clamped, lethargy and lack of appetite.
Treatment: Manufacturers claim that some anti-ulcer treatments are effective against septicaemia.

Ulcers
Ulcers on the outside of the fish, especially if only one or two fish are infected, are generally a secondary infection from smaller wounds caused by predators, handling or parasites. Bacteria settle in even small scratches in the mucous layer of the fish. Once the bacteria become established and an ulcer develops, then the ulcer will release further bacteria into the environment, putting the rest of the fish population at risk of infection.

Interior ulcers are caused by bacteria in the blood stream of the fish, which produce raised areas that will suddenly burst out into open sores. These are very infectious.

Treatment: In the early stages, bactericides are effective as are specific anti-ulcer treatments. For severe infections, combine a bactericide treatment with a salt bath. Isolate severely-infected fish in good conditions. Sometimes a colony of parasitic protozoan or trematode worms feeds on the edge of the wound, making it difficult to heal. Therefore, a treatment containing anti-parasite and anti-fungal agents is necessary.

Pond salt is very beneficial for fish with ulcer problems, as it slows down the loss of body fluids through any lesions. If too much fluid is lost, kidney failure might result. Use 3g/l if possible. In an emergency case, isolate the victim and treat in a bath at 9g/l for 15 minutes. This concentration is the equivalent to that of the salts of its own bodily fluids.

Bacterial Diseases of the Gills and Dropsy
These conditions cause the fish to become very bloated to the extent that its scales stick out like pine cones.
Treatment: The advice used to be that infected fish were humanely disposed of. Nowadays, some manufacturers claim that their anti-ulcer treatments are effective against internal bacteria. This is worth trying in isolation. Sometimes the bacterial infection is a secondary infection caused by parasitic infestation, the parasites having taken advantage of a stressed or weakened host. See the table at the end of the chapter for a list of the parastitic symptoms, fish behaviour, and possible treatments.

Viruses
Viruses can be highly infectious in high populations and as cooler conditions suppress fish immune systems. They may also be spread by parasites. There is no known cure for them at the moment.
Carp Pox or Cyprinoid Herpes Virus: Solid waxy lumps appear on fins, body and mouth. Usually they appear in times of stress and abate as conditions improve.
Spring Viraemia of Carp: Bloated body, like dropsy. This is a result of the body filling with fluid and the liver and spleen swelling. Pale gills with bleeding under the skin. Prevention is the only cure. Contamination can occur from tainted water, equipment or the fish louse or leeches.

Untreatable Ailments

There are many more diseases, viruses and parasites. If the proprietary treatments have no effect, then the fish should be humanely disposed of.

Some 'untreatable' ailments can be rectified with antibiotics and drugs that are available only on prescription from your veterinary surgeon. These must be administered exactly according to instructions after an expert and qualified diagnosis, and are generally the last action taken by the keen Koi carp keeper. Happily, many of the above complaints rarely infect or affect your run-of-the-mill goldfish.

Further Precautions to Avoid Disease

1. Cleanliness and water quality and no overcrowding (see *Fish Problems*, page 36). Diseases thrive in water of poor quality. The stress on the fish caused by the poor water quality reduces their natural immunity.
2. Buy fish only from a reputable dealer and at the right time of year.
3. Quarantine your new acquisitions for at least 10 days in a specially-prepared small pool where they can be well cared for.

4. Handle with care.
5. Feed good-quality food only when the water temperature is above 8°C (45°F) and only what the fish will eat in 5 minutes.
6. Remove dead and dying fish as soon as you spot them.

Other Non-Life Threatening Fish Problems

Symptoms: Twisted spine; bent fish.
Cause: Electric shocks (for example, lightning), fright or stress, or overdoses of medication.
Treatment: None.

Some ornamentals contract **swim bladder infections** which never become life threatening but leave them forever swimming like a frogman with a life jacket on.

Parasites

Parasitic Symptoms	Behaviour	Treatment after Chemical Check
Lernaea Anchor worm: thread 2cm long protruding from swelling		Anti-parasite dose Salt baths effective on young worms
Slimy skin Chinodella – excess mucous	bluish hue clamped fins respiratory distress depression	Anti-parasite or salt bath 3g/l
Epistylis or Heteropolaria White fuzzy patches, progress to form ulcers in the skin. Secondary infection and septicaemia		Check that it is not Saprolegnia (fungus) Anti-parasite salt bath 22g/l for weeks. 30 mins every 7 days for 3 weeks
Dactylogyrus and Gyrodactylus Flukes, ulcers loss of colour pallid gills	sluggish	Anti-parasite dose. 10 days later use an anti-bactericide. Alternatively, salt bath.

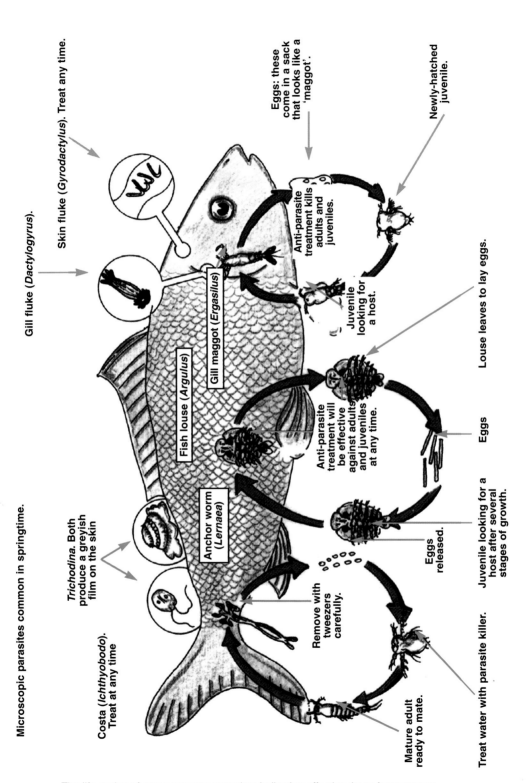

Gill fluke (*Dactylogyrus*).

Skin fluke (*Gyrodactylus*). Treat any time.

Microscopic parasites common in springtime.

Trichodina. Both produce a greyish film on the skin

Costa (*Ichthyobodo*). Treat at any time

Fish louse (*Argulus*)

Gill maggot (*Ergasilus*)

Anchor worm (*Lernaea*)

Eggs: these come in a sack that looks like a 'maggot'.

Newly-hatched juvenile.

Anti-parasite treatment kills adults and juveniles.

Juvenile looking for a host.

Louse leaves to lay eggs.

Anti-parasite treatment will be effective against adults and juveniles at any time.

Eggs

Eggs released.

Juvenile looking for a host after several stages of growth.

Remove with tweezers carefully.

Treat water with parasite killer.

Mature adult ready to mate.

The life cycles of some common parasites indicating effective times for treatment.

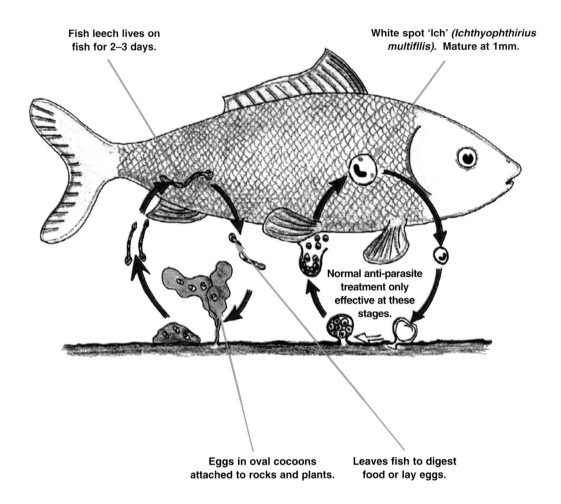

Fish leech lives on fish for 2–3 days.

White spot 'Ich' *(Ichthyophthirius multifllis).* Mature at 1mm.

Normal anti-parasite treatment only effective at these stages.

Eggs in oval cocoons attached to rocks and plants.

Leaves fish to digest food or lay eggs.

More common parasites.

Argulus Fish lice, ulcers, especially around the gills.		Quarantine new fish in treatment tank or pond. Salt baths effective on young lice.
Gill maggots (Ergasilus)	fish breathing rapidly emaciated	Anti-parasite dose or 3g/1l salt bath. Touch with weak solution of iodine or potassium permanganate.

Leeches: worm-like with suckering disc each end.		Anti-parasite dose or 3g/1l salt at bath. Touch with weak solution of iodine or pot. permanganate.
Ichtyobodo necator or **Costia necatrix** Excess mucous, skin reddened with pale gills covered in thick mucus. Fungus is often a secondary invader.	loss of appetite clamped fins	Anti-parasite dose Treat pond with salt or anti-bacterial medication.
Ichthyophthirius multifillis 'White spot' or 'Ich' White spots sharply defined all over the body.	twitching and scraping	Anti-parasite dose twice, 48 hours apart for 7 days if below 60°C. If fish removed from the pond after 7 days, it will be free of parasites.
Molluscs' glocchidia: parasite; immature stage of freshwater molluscs. Irritation, slight risk of secondary infection after the glocchidia leave their host. Tiny brown spots.		Will drop off on own accord. Possible treatment for ulcers.
Trichodina: after excess mucous, body surface covered in dry cells. Fungus is often a secondary invader.	leaps out of water hangs at surface gulps for air	Anti-parasite dose. Reduce stress.
Wasting disease		Can be internal parasites. May be TB (see *Untreatable Ailments*). Anti-parasite and vitamins.
Wounds from accidents or other causes. Trematode worms feeding on the wound.		Treat the wound with a chemical specifically for secondary infections.

CHAPTER SEVEN
CONSERVATION OR 'NATURAL' PONDS

The problems inherent in the design of conservation ponds make them worthy of a separate chapter. It is not that they are more prone to problems, it is just that a problem of any sort is more difficult to correct. Bearing in mind that a pond is attempting to evolve into a boggy place – a hole filled with detritus – we must also bear in mind that conservation ponds are much more dynamic at being able to achieve this.

Why?

First, they start with a minimum of 10cm (4in) of mud on the bottom.

Second, the mud 'kick-starts' the cycle of life into motion so quickly that it seems that no sooner have you turned your back on the thing then in an instant it is full of plants and goodness knows what. If the plants are given full rein in the pond, that is, are not restrained in baskets, then the rampant and voracious character of the main body of water and marginal plants is instantly revealed. So, just cleaning out the pond becomes a problem, apart from any others that might occur.

Having said all that, my experience with conservation ponds, particularly if they are very large, is that they are a lot less problematic in the ecological sense. Disease and water quality problems seem to be less apparent, perhaps because of the steadying effect of the much more vibrant living environment.

Tips for Clearing and Cleaning Conservation Ponds

Safety Precautions

1. Make sure your tetanus injections are up to date.
2. Make yourself familiar with the contours of the bottom of the pond. Check where there are any sumps or drop-offs. If there are any very deep areas of mud in which you may have to work, you can make a platform of corrugated iron as a sort of duckboard. This is particularly useful if you do not intend to drain the pond, but remember to attach a piece of rope to it so that you can retrieve it when you have finished.
3. Always wear thick-soled boots. Pull out rubbish with tools. Wear gloves. Don't wear waders if you are working by yourself.
4. Have extra spare, warm, dry clothes to hand, particularly in winter. Change into them at the end of the day – people will like you a lot more!
5. Keep your back straight and don't overdo it lifting out heavy shovelfuls of slime.

Tools

For the larger project the basic tool is a muck rake, manure drag or crome for clearing aquatic weeds. You will also need a billhook, very old pruning saw, old carving knife and grass hook and shovel. Needless to say, care must be taken if the pool is lined with a flexible liner when using these tools.

For the smaller pond, you will also need pumping or siphoning equipment, such as a large bore hose and possibly a pump that will take thickly-muddied water and a certain amount of solids. Buckets and a water supply and hose for washing down and refill are useful. A plastic dust pan and brush are perfect for cleaning out the last few gallons of slimy water in a lined pool.

Cleaning Out Conservation Ponds

If the pond is large, then many hands make light work. The aim is to (a) dig; (b) transport and (c) dispose of the muck and rubbish in the pond. (See also *Overgrown ponds*, pages 62–63.)

Dig:
- To start with, find the original bottom of the pond. Then work from one or two definite points on the bank.
- If the pond is clay lined and you have to drain it, make sure the clay stays moist. Start work on a humid day and drape the sides in plastic.
- Most rooted plants grow from rhizomes. These must be completely cleaned out or they will resprout. Carefully cut around the edge of a patch of marginal plants, then lever it gently. It should then float off and can be dragged to the side. Leave plant material to drain on the bank for a while. This allows small animals the chance to escape back into the water. If there is a huge mat of plants, then a number of people working in a line is the best way to clear it.
- When it comes to clearing the real mud, silt and rubbish on the bottom of the pond, start at the bank and work out into the pond, so that you are not churning up the mud and silt or tripping over the rubbish that you are about to remove.
- For deep ponds, a log winched across the bottom gathers in a lot of silt that can be disposed of more easily close to the bank.

Transporting the rubbish out of the pond:
- Sometimes a chain-gang system is the most effective, as climbing in and out of the pond can be very tiring or even hazardous.
- If you are barrowing or moving material out of the pond, make the incline of any plankways as shallow as possible. Support planks at both ends and in the middle. Standard builder's scaffolding planks need to be placed two-wide. A three-wide plank run is ideal. Batton the planks for grip or, alternatively, tack a spiral of rope in place. Heavy barrows can be pulled with ropes hooked to the front of the barrows whilst being pushed from behind – an old navvy technique.
- If the job is a large one, work methodically on a small area at a time. Work as a team. A smooth cycle is better than a burst of activity followed by halts. A circular pattern is better than a linear one. Full buckets or barrows go out by one route as empty ones come in by another.
- If you are leaving material to drain on the bank and allow small animals to escape, be careful not to smother large areas of bank and not to leave silt where it will run back into the pond.

Disposal:
- Make a separate pile for real rubbish such as broken glass, and skip it.
- Sludge can grow over but be careful that it does not wash back. Reeds can be dumped to rot off or dry out.

At the end of the day:
- Clean and grease up your tools.

Cleaning out natural or conservation ponds

firm support

Corrugated iron as duckboarding. Rope attached to
assist removal from the bankside.

Cutting and pulling: breaking up large clumps of marginals with rutter
(peat knife) and crome or muck hack (muck rake).

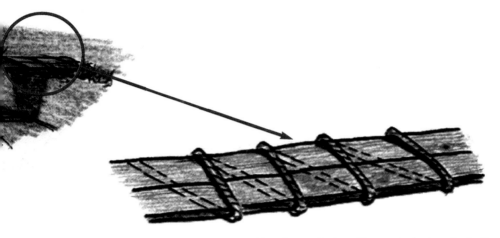

Treadway: planks with rope tacked or stapled in
a spiral. Alternatively use battens.

bankside of pool   Hook and rope to help with the haulage.

support

Support

Shallow incline made with planks battened together
and oil drum (clean one that does not leak).

Choice of Plants for the 'Natural' Pond

Here are a range of typical and indigenous water plants that are suitable for new conservation ponds or lakes. You may come across a few other reeds and rushes but, in a domestic situation or in an area where you might want to exercise some control, these might run rampant.

Where I feel the plant deserves particular consideration because of its attractiveness and reserved behaviour, I have marked it with an asterisk (*).

If I feel the plant is constantly on the verge of misbehaviour and should only be considered for the larger lakeside, I have labelled it with an exclamation mark (!).

Plants that are not really indigenous but are firmly established in the country I have marked with a question mark (?).

1. Small bankside plants and emergent plants such as small marginals could be considered as ground cover around the water's edge and in the water itself, blending the margins:
    *   *Caltha palustris* (King Cup or Marsh Marigold)
        Lysimachia nummularia (Creeping Jenny)
    !   *Mentha aquatica* (Water Mint)
        Menyanthes trifoliata (Bog Bean) Not for very shallow margins.
    *   *Mimulus guttatus/luteus* (Monkey Musk) Seeds itself everywhere.
    *   *Myosotis palustris* (Water Forget-me-not) Seeds itself everywhere.
    !   *Potentilla palustria* (Marsh Cinquefoil) Rampant in certain circumstances.
        Veronica beccabunga (Brooklime)

2. Larger plants, exclusively emergent, such as marginals up to their 'necks' in water.
    *   *Acorus calamus* (Sweet Flag) Variegated version is less vigorous.
        Alisma plantago aquatica (Great Water Plantain)
    *   *Butomus umbellatus* (Flowering Rush)
    !   *Carex riparia* (Great Pond Sedge)
    ?   *Cotula coronipifolia* (Golden Buttons)
    !   *Cyperus longus* (Sweet Galingale)
        Eriophorum angustifolium (Cotton Grass) Ever popular.
    !   *Glyceria maxima* (Reed Sweet Grass) Even the variegated form can be rampant.
    *   *Iris pseudacorus* (Yellow Flag) A must for every water garden, but don't turn your back on it for too long.
    *! *Lythrum salicaria* (Purple Loosestrife) Can be tenacious if well established. A problem plant in the USA.
    !   *Juncus effussus* (Soft Rush)
    !   *Phalaris arundinacea* (Reed Canary Grass)
    !! *Phragmites communis*
        Ranunculus lingua grandiflora (Greater Spearwort)
    !   *Rorippa nasturtium officianale* (Nasturtium Officianale/Water Cress) Rampant but useful for keeping the water clean, particularly in a reed bed filtration unit. However, it is susceptible to polluted water.
        Rorippa microphylla (Water Cress) Similar to above but larger flowers and less seed.

Marsh Marigold *(Caltha palustris)*

Water Forget-me-not *(Myosotis palustris)*

Brooklime *(Veronica beccabunga)*

Yellow Flag Iris *(Iris pseudacorus)*

Attractive native marginal area plants with reserved habits.

?! *Sagittaria latifolia* (Arrowhead)
! *Scirpus lacustris* (This is the true Bulrush) Beware! Once established, it is very tenacious.
! *Sparganium erectum* (Bur-reed)
! *Typha angustifolia* (Lesser Reedmace) Not as vigorous as *latifolia*.
!! *Typha latifolia* (Reedmace) Most people think of this as the Bulrush. Beware!
* *Typha minima* (Least Reedmace) Ideal for the small pond.

3. Deep water plants with leaves to the surface.
    Nuphar lutea (Yellow Water Lily)
    Nymphaea alba (White Water Lily)
    Polygonum amphibium (Amphibious Persicaria) Not very deep water.
    Ranunculus aquatalis (Common Water Crowfoot) There are several very similar varieties. It functions partly as an oxygenator from its submerged leaves.

4. Floating plants.
    Hydrocharis morsus ranae (Frogbit)
! *Lemna minor* (Duckweed)
! *Lemna trisulca* (Ivy Leafed Duckweed)
    Stratiotes aloides (Water Soldier)

Marginals   **Deep water plants**   **Floating plants**

**Water Soldier
(*Stratiotes aloides*)**

**Yellow Water Lily
(*Nuphar lutea*)**

**Flowering Rush
(*Butomus umbellatus*)**

Water Plantain (*Alisma plantago aquatica*) **White Water Lily (*Nymphaea alba*)** **Frogbit (*Hydrocharis morsus ranae*)**

More desirable native water plants.

5. Submerged oxygenating plants.
    Callitriche verna (Starwort)
    Ceratophyllum demersum (Hornwort)
!   *Chara species* (Stonewort)
!? *Elodea candensis* (Canadian Pondweed) Also known as Anacharis.
?   *Elodea crispa* (Curly Pondweed, as is *Lagarosiphon major*) The best oxygenator and easy to control.
    Groenlandia densa (Opposite Leaved Pondweed) Streams to ponds.
    Houttynia palustria (Water Violet)
    Largarosiphon major See *Elodea crispa.*
!   *Myriophyllum spicatus* (Water Milfoil)
    Potamageton species (Curled Pondweed) Loves calcerious streams, especially crispa.
    Ranunculus aquatalis (Water Crowfoot) See marginals.
    Rorippa (Watercress) See marginals.

Choice of Fish

Fish are usually of a secondary concern in the conservation pond, so there is generally no environmental pressure from the over-population of fish. Natural triggers control their success and survival and they take their place in the larger scheme of things. If you overstock, it is more difficult to control the situation with any chemical treatments. Also, the choice of fish needs some consideration to avoid problems. Ideally, choose indigenous species.

Barbel may be predatory and they need plenty of oxygen.
Bream make water cloudy.
Carp make water cloudy. Keep separate from bream.
Chubb are very predatory.
Grass carp eat plants, grow large and have a tendency to jump out.
Gudgeon or Stone Loach need clean, fine gravel substrate, oxygen and moving water. They bully smaller fish.
Minnows need to shoal, will be eaten by larger fish, and need plenty of oxygen.
Perch are carnivorous and aggressive; they upset other species.
Pike You must be nuts! But, having said that, if you have too many fish of any particular variety, what better natural control is there?
Roach and Rudd are ideal.
Sterlet need clean substrate to sift through, cold water and a large quantity of food. They are suitable for large pools only.
Sticklebacks will harass and damage fish much larger than themselves.
Tench stir up the mud in some pools as they forage on the bottom for their food, which is mostly caddisfly larvae and bottom-dwelling grubs. (Contrary to popular belief, they are not nature's vacuum cleaners.)
Trout need masses of oxygen and gravel bottom. The water needs to be crystal clear as they are visual feeders. They also need 2m (6.5ft) of depth, and should never be mixed with carp.

Anti-social pond residents

Great Diving Beetle
(Dysticus Marginalis)

female has striped back

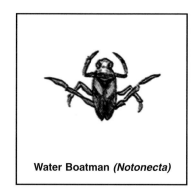

Water Boatman *(Notonecta)*

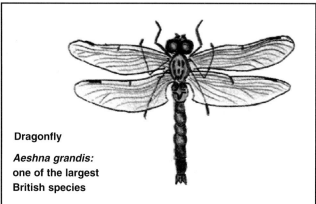

Dragonfly

Aeshna grandis:
one of the largest
British species

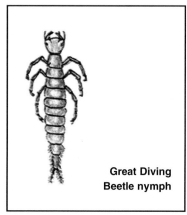

**Great Diving
Beetle nymph**

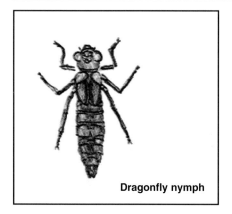

Dragonfly nymph

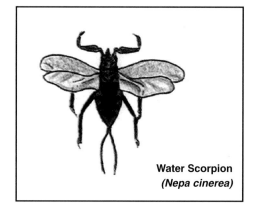

Water Scorpion
(Nepa cinerea)

Approximate actual size

Unwanted guests

fore foot

rear foot

stool or spore

mink

heron

grass snake

Animal pests and predators can be divided into (a) antisocial pond residents; and (b) unwanted guests.

Antisocial Pond Residents

Ignore the little beetles, the problem is the Great Diving Beetle, *Dysticus marginalis*. This kills small fish which are considerably larger than itself. Net it out. It is not to be confused with the Great Silver Beetle which eats plants and is the largest beetle in the pond. The Great Diving Beetle has a paler brown margin around the edge of its shell.

Waterboatmen (*Notonecta*, four species) are sometimes referred to as Backswimmers to distinguish them from the Lesser Waterboatmen (*Corixa*, 36 species). They attack very small fry and damage larger fish. Net them out if they are present in large numbers. The Backswimmers are also distinctive because they swim upside down. They have longer, more pointed, backs than *Corixa*.

Water Lily Beetle (*Galerucella nymphaea*) is dull brown and slightly larger than a ladybird. The juvenile is a hump-backed grub. Both the grub and the adult feed on lily leaves by cutting channels in the surface. Eventually the channels merge and the leaf blackens and decays. (See also page 74.)

Water scorpions (*Nepa cinerea* and *Ranatra linearis*) are frightening to look at, with their legs adapted to look and serve as giant mandibles, but they are harmless to all but the smallest of pond creatures.

Dragonfly larvae eat fish fry. Live with it.

Frogs have been known to grab largish fish or fat, slow ornamentals whilst in the grip of spring fever. There is no real risk; write a letter to your local paper if you see it happen. Fat, slow ornamentals ought to be indoors at frog spawning time.

Mosquitoes and their larvae thrive without competition and in very stagnant ponds. You may have a water problem. Get some more plant life in there. Fish soon eat all mosquito larvae, but they won't tolerate stagnant conditions.

Newts eat fish fry but are good guys really. The Great Crested Newt is a protected species.

Snails eat plants. *Planorbis corneus*, the large Ramshorn, is preferable to *Linnaea stagnalis*. You will find their eggs under lily leaves. Rub them off. (See also *Plant Problems: Eaten Foliage*, page 74.)

These animals are all part of the fabric of the environment and, unless their numbers get ludicrously out of control, they will find their niche in the exciting cycle of life in the pond. If they do seem to be thriving at the expense of the rest of the pond community, then they must be thriving on something that is itself thriving.

Unwanted Guests

There is 'nowt so queer as folk', and there is no human so protective of anything in the world than the Koi-keeping fish enthusiast of his prize Koi carp. A Koi keeper will have nurtured his precious pisces through bad times and good, very often in conditions that make the average swimming pool look like a septic tank. With a capital outlay for a pool and filter system often running well into five figures and the estimated value of the occupants sometimes matching that easily, then you can see there are some very serious people around willing to pay anything to guard against predators. Cats are the Koi keepers' four-footed enemy number one, and herons are the main biped pest.

If money is no object, then technology provides a never-ending array of possibilities. But what is relevant to us of more modest means and simpler water gardens? Also, we love our furry four-footed friends and feathered chums and we like to have them around – sometimes. But it would be nice to know that when we leave the tranquil scene murder and mayhem are not the next items on the agenda!

Herons and Cats

There is an old adage: 'Curiosity killed the cat.' Cats have been with us since time immemorial. The convenience of having man as the provider of sustenance, either directly or indirectly, keeps a good population of moggies thriving in all communities around the world. As a result, they have time on their paws; time to lie back and watch the busy world stream by. In the same way that we spend hours watching the world on television, the cat happily watches the world in a hole with water in it. It's just as dramatic and more interactive than television. At the moment, the television can only be switched on or off, or the sound turned up and down. But, with a pool, if you really like something, you can hook it out!

It is curiosity that gets cats going to begin with. If you can catch them at an early stage, then you might be able to prevent a problem developing, based on the old saying: 'A scalded cat fears cold water' (or something like that). Or, from an old Somerset gardener I knew years ago: 'If you catch 'e doin' it, just boot the bugger in!'

Early action reinforces the message, resulting in the situation referred to in another old saying: 'The cat loves fish but dares not wet her paws.'

In general, cats hate water and hate getting wet if they are dry. If dunking them in the water seems to be taking the philosophy of 'being cruel to be kind' too far, or the animal disappears more rapidly that you can act, arm yourself with one of those 'mega-blaster-supa-squirter' water-pistols. Then dealing with the problem becomes fun.

This, of course, is no deterrent to the heron, who is the epitome of patience. The

Look at it this way ...

Cats need to be persuaded to keep away from ponds...

...for their own good!

heron will wait unseen until it knows that you are not in the vicinity. It is intelligent enough to learn the routine of when you are about, when you get up, when you go to work, and so on. If you change the routine, that is when you catch it unawares. When you do see it next to your pond, you will probably have a strong sense of receiving mixed blessings, since you cannot help feeling that it is a privilege to see something so graceful so close to home.

But we cannot be forever patrolling our water garden territory and, if we are constantly being raided by a horde of wayward moggies, there are some very simple, practical measures that we can take to help the fish to help themselves, such as providing a fish hide in the form of a concrete slab on the bottom of the pond raised up on bricks or large bore pipes laid on the bottom.

Zap 'Em or Blast 'Em

What is there on the garden centre shelves that is manufactured specifically to cater for the feline or heron problem? The products that actually protect the pond rather than just alert you to an intruder boil down to shock, in the form of electricity, or annoyance in the form of an earpiercing (to the cat – inaudible to humans and, unfortunately, herons) high-frequency noise.

'Catwatch' is an electronic cat deterrent that produces an ultra-sound triggered off by body heat. Each small unit protects a 100-degree swathe of some 42 sq m (450 sq ft). It is also good for protecting birds, as the noise is inaudible to them. However, that is bad news for those of us looking for a dual-purpose cat-and-heron scarer.

'Scarecrow' is a heat-activated device that, when confronted by a warm body, bursts into life, chattering, rattling dementedly and spraying a jet of water in an arc over all and sundry within 30ft. This combines all the ingredients necessary to inhibit all unwelcome visitors except children. Kids will love it.

'Pondguard' heron scarer is specifically marketed as a heron scarer. It consists of an extended trip line which a heron cannot avoid touching as it approaches a pool. When the line is touched, there is a startling bang from a percussive cap, accompanied by a device that suddenly flashes a pair of eyes in a cat-shaped silhouette. A cat would probably get wise to it eventually, and it needs to be reset every time it goes off. But that one big fright might be enough to do the trick permanently, and then you are left with a dynamic conversation piece at your midsummer barbecue, although somehow I don't think the neighbours will be that impressed with it.

As we get into the realms of serious problem-solving devices, we are left with the 'Pond Protection Kit'. This takes us back to the 'cruel to be kind' philosophy as it consists of surrounding your pond with an electric fence. Wilf Starsmore, the inventor, has made his concept a reality without making the pool look too much like Stalag 17. The poly wires carry a small current, just enough to deter and not to maim, and are suspended in little looped rods just above the water level. It can be powered by battery or mains and costs about £4.00 a year to run. Best of all, it does the job – and no messing!

The simplest purchase has to be the joke snake recommended by Alan Titchmarsh (Gardener's World, BBC1). Take one rubber snake, curl it up as though it were nonchalantly passing the time of day and place it in a strategic part of the garden. Hey presto! Garden minus cats.

Otters and Mink

Otters are not a problem; they are another privilege. If you don't like otters in your garden, I am sure there is someone who does, and you could sell your house to them. Alternatively, rent it out to a television Natural History unit.

Mink are a different proposition. Try to work out where they might be coming from (generally they live near waterways). Contact the relevant warden or gamekeeper for that area, who will be more than willing to help all he can. Even if the mink are actually living on your land, many fisheries and game wardens will be keen to trap or shoot them in order to deal with the problem before it spreads to their land or waterways.

Mink are not really the problem that many people have made them out to be but, if you have them raiding your pond, this is not something you will feel convinced about. If you don't live very near a waterway or river, and your pond has been ransacked just the once, then it may be the work of a transitory male on the move over the countryside looking for a territory. Mink won't settle on a small pond, as they need several miles of river bank to feel at home.

Designing a child-safe pond or making an established pond 'child safe'.

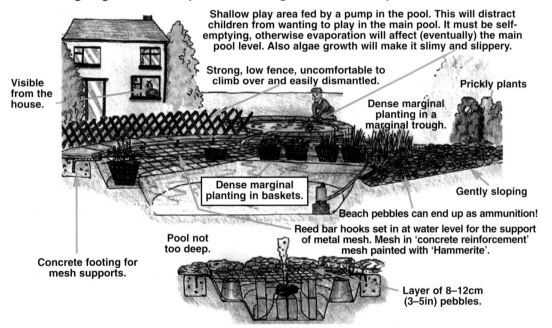

Shallow play area fed by a pump in the pool. This will distract children from wanting to play in the main pool. It must be self-emptying, otherwise evaporation will affect (eventually) the main pool level. Also algae growth will make it slimy and slippery.

Strong, low fence, uncomfortable to climb over and easily dismantled.

Visible from the house.

Prickly plants

Dense marginal planting in a marginal trough.

Dense marginal planting in baskets.

Gently sloping

Beach pebbles can end up as ammunition!

Pool not too deep.

Reed bar hooks set in at water level for the support of metal mesh. Mesh in 'concrete reinforcement' mesh painted with 'Hammerite'.

Concrete footing for mesh supports.

Layer of 8–12cm (3–5in) pebbles.

A child-safe pool created from an established pre-formed pool. 5cm (2in) mesh (stainless or painted with Hammerite) supported by hooks, blocks and upturned pots. Raised pump pushes water through a gushing, foaming fountain jet.

Children

There is no solution to the problems children can cause unless you design the landscape with them in mind. Work with the children and educate them. However, if you have toddlers around, you have to create a child-safe pool.

If you have inherited a pool by moving house and you have very young children, fill it in or fence it. This need not be permanent; in fact you could still use it to work a fountain feature. But bear in mind that where there is water and children, children generally end up in the water, quite often head first. Don't just drain the pool and leave it empty and expect it to stay empty, even if it is made of cracked old concrete.

A grid of 10cm (4in) of galvanised or painted weldmesh (used for reinforcing concrete) hooked immovably into place just below the water surface works effectively. The plants will grow up through the mesh undeterred and animals can get in and out of the pond quite happily. It is an expensive solution but a compromise that allows the pond to continue to function undisturbed until the child population becomes more responsible.

Mice, Bank Voles (Water Rats), and Moles

These have all proved themselves to be nuisances to someone at some time. Where they have undermined lined pools and ponds and even holed the liner, it may be necessary eventually to put a thin concrete skin underneath.

New pond liners can be laid on sand with a 'lean mix' of cement dust (8:1) in with it. This gradually hardens as it absorbs the moisture from the surrounding earth and will foil any potential mining activities under the liner.

Immediate remedial response has been smoke bombs and vibrators clicking away in the soil, or traps.

Snakes

In Britain, if you see a snake swimming in your pond, it is almost certainly a grass snake. It is completely harmless to everything except amphibians and small fish. It is probably nesting in your compost heap. If you have an abject fear of snakes and desperately need to get rid of it, contact a local animal welfare group or conservation body which may help you to relocate it.

Landscaping Techniques to Discourage Predators

If we were in the fortunate position of being able to capitalise on hindsight and were able to re-landscape our water garden effortlessly, we might take a page out of the Victorians' book, where the water level was at least 15cm (6in) below the pond edging and designed as such. This solves the problem of cats and herons.

A low wall that doubles as a seat keeps cats out of reach of the water. However, you must make it possible for small wildlife to get in and out of the pond. I was once commissioned to make such a wall into a toad hotel, with sitting-rooms, dining rooms and bedrooms; of course, the bathroom was communal!

It might be less bother to have a low picket fence. This is not as comfortable to sit on, but does help to keep children safe, who are another ingredient that doesn't mix with water.

A rock edge next to the pool could be deep enough to keep meddlesome paws away from water level.

A wreath of spiky, thorny plants, particularly when planted amongst rocks or gravel, is visually effective. Berberis have red, yellow or green leaves, and come large or small, deciduous or evergreen and have stunning yellow or orange flowers. Once established as an impenetrable thicket, the soil beneath becomes a 'no-go' area of discarded thorns. *Ulex* (common gorse), in the not-so-common forms of *Ulex galli* and *Ulex flore pleno* (Plenus) make neat, uncomfortable hummocks. Again, you are stuck with yellow.

For an endless variety of stunning colour that will cover everywhere and make it impenetrable for pussies are the roses, especially those classified as ground cover roses. My particular favourites are among the 'County' series.

The pool planting itself can help, as there is nothing to hinder pussy predators more than a good, solid planting of marginal plants in baskets just below the water surface. Unfortunately, this is excellent cover for the heron.

Endnote

I am reminded of one of the ponds I built at Clacks Farm of TV fame. The pond in question was a raised pre-formed pool with a crazy paving surround, perfect for the two cats, GetOut and StayOut, to bask in the sunshine and pass the time fishing. After I had built the ponds and tested the fountains and waterfalls, I left the local handyman/electrician to wire up the pumps to the household mains. When I came back several weeks later for the first Open Day of the summer, I was keen to make sure all the ponds looked right and that the fountains worked. I was quite surprised to see the same half-a-dozen small fish we had left there earlier in the year still resident and thriving. GetOut and StayOut had laid off!

Anyway, the fountain pump pre-filter needed cleaning so I stuck my hand in to drag it out. I got such a shock that I thought someone had kicked me in the arm and leg at the same time. That was why those fish had survived – the electrician had wired the pumps in such a way that they were making the water live. I can tell you, after that I always think twice about sticking my hand in a pool, and I think GetOut and StayOut do too, don't you? (NB. That was in the days before installation of RCDs or RCCBs was standard practice.)

Ideas for deterring predators.

Ultra-sonic cat deterrent or alarm for any intruder.

This device squirts water at anything in the vicinity.

The device snaps open with a loud bang.

the boot

thorny plants

Access for amphibians

Rubber snake hidden in the grass.

Trip wires are effective by themselves. They can also be used to operate noise machines or give an electric shock.

Fish hides and old bits of pipe.

Raised pool edge above water level or lowered water level.

Plenty of marginal plants and deep water plants for cover.

CHAPTER NINE
OVERGROWN PONDS

Once 7–10cm (3–4in) of detritus has built up in the bottom of a pond, it is time to think in terms of cleaning out. For particularly large ponds various products, such as 'Aquaplankton', stimulate a massive growth of bacterial activity that can be very effective at digesting huge quantities of organic matter lying on the bottom of the pond. These products need oxygen and heat to work so, if the pond is lacking in oxygenators, mechanical or botanical, and autumn is on the horizon, then there is no avoiding the evil day – the big clean out.

Late summer/early autumn is, in fact, the best time to clean out: best for you because the water is still warm; best for the wildlife which has not yet begun to look for winter resting places; best for the plants if you want to divide them successfully in time for the spring display.

Tools and Equipment

General
- Pump capable of pumping thick, muddy water. Large-bore hose suitable for the pump and siphoning.
- Buckets.
- Plastic dust pan and brush. A very coarse brush is essential for cleaning pool sides.
- Water supply and hose for washing down and refilling.

Splitting Plants
- A polythene ground sheet.
- Containers for floating plants and deep water aquatics, also for marginals if it is warm. This is unlikely, and damp newspapers will do.
- Two garden forks or a garden knife. Also scissors, secateurs and trowel.
- All the necessary ingredients for replanting: fresh soil, possibly new baskets, hessians and topping gravel.

Storing Fish
- Holding container and cover net. Find a place in the shade for the fish and do not feed them.
- Air pump for aeration.
- Catching net.
- Tap water conditioner.

Method
1. Save as much of the clean water from the surface of the pond as possible. Use this to store the fish, and as a starter for the 'aging' of the water in the pool when you top up with fresh water.
2. Whilst the pond is emptying, busy yourself by removing the plants and dividing them. You might find that it is necessary to divide them *in situ* just so that you can get them out. (If this is the case with particular varieties, then be wary of putting too much of this material back into the pond.) When I am struggling with the hippo-like proportions of

some reeds or rushes, I find an old pruning saw or strong old carving knife indispensable, but take great care, especially in a pond that has a flexible plastic or rubber liner, that the blade does not slip.

Carve the plant material away from the original container. Don't be too brutal with it as for some plants, especially irises and lilies, this is the best and most lively material for propagating the plant. You may have some difficulty in extracting the plant from its original container. In this instance, it is your decision whether to let sleeping dogs lie and return the plant in its original container having given it just a 'short back and sides', or increase, replenish and divide. (See also Chapter 10, *Propagating Plants.*) Here you turn into Sweeney Todd; throwing all caution to the wind, you brutalise the planting basket for its contents to use for your own ends.

3.   Catch the fish when the pond is almost empty. Although it seems stressful for them to be slithering around in the mud, it is a lot less so than being chased vainly around the pond by a madman with a net, and still end up slithering around in the mud. Take this opportunity to check each fish, store it separately in a hospital tank with a salt water bath as a tonic, or with a dose of the specific chemical treatment for the problem. Cover and aerate the tank or containers. Do not feed the fish.

4.   Continue to drain the pool as far as possible, checking all the time for tiddlers.

5.   Use the dust pan and bucket for the last remaining gallons of water and detritus. This will be greatly appreciated on the compost heap or flower beds.

6.   Rinse down and brush off any excessive blanket weed. Do not use detergents. Some experts recommend painting any tenacious strands with algicide.

7.   Even if this endeavour is nothing to do with pool liner repairs, it is a good idea to check the liner at this point anyway. In particular, check the seams and just above the water line.

8.   Try to start filling up as soon as possible, adding the required amount of dechlorinator to the water. Top up with the remains of the pool water if the fish are not in it. If they are, and they seem happy, it may be as well to let the water stand for 2–3 hours whilst the dechlorinator does its job.

9.   Whilst the pond is filling, continue to divide and repot the plants.

10. Return any floating plants.

11. Return the fish, acclimatising them to the water by floating them in plastic bags part-filled with their pond water. Roll down the tops of the plastic bags to form floats. Leave the temperature to adjust to that of the pond by leaving the bags to float for 20 minutes. Every few minutes, add a few ccs of pond water so that the fish can acclimatise to the chemical nature of their new habitat.

12. Only feed the fish very sparingly at first. Do not add any new fish until the pond has completely recovered, in other words, if you clean out in the late summer, do not get any more fish until the following spring.

Ornamental marginals blending with the bog garden backdrop and a deeper water planting. It is rather like any perennial or herbaceous border.

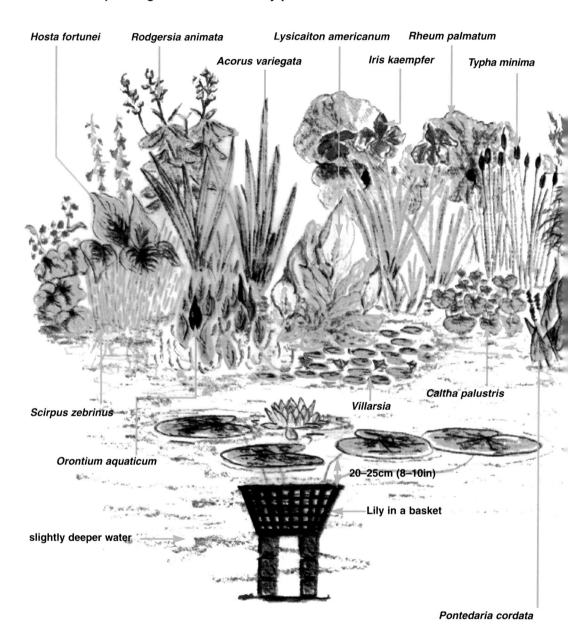

Hosta fortunei

Rodgersia animata

Acorus variegata

Lysicaiton americanum

Iris kaempfer

Rheum palmatum

Typha minima

Scirpus zebrinus

Orontium aquaticum

Villarsia

Caltha palustris

20–25cm (8–10in)

Lily in a basket

slightly deeper water

Pontedaria cordata

Water lilies need still water. Start them off fairly shallow and gradually lower them over a period. Different lilies prefer specific depths.

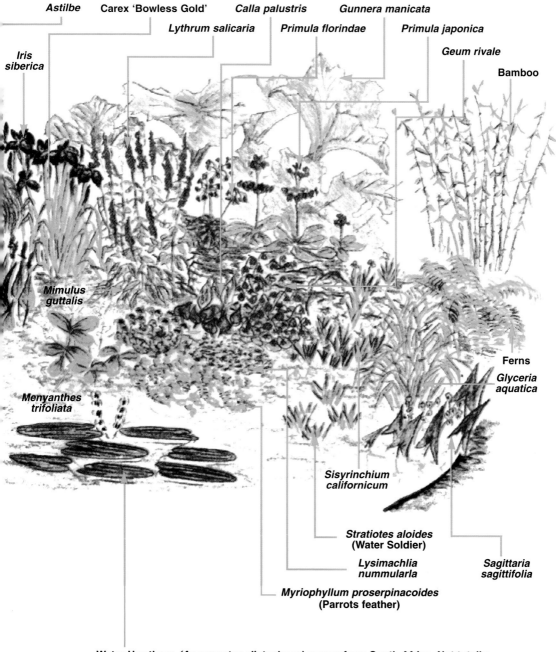

Astilbe

Carex 'Bowless Gold'

Calla palustris

Gunnera manicata

Lythrum salicaria

Primula florindae

Primula japonica

Iris siberica

Geum rivale

Bamboo

Mimulus guttalis

Ferns

Glyceria aquatica

Menyanthes trifoliata

Sisyrinchium californicum

Stratiotes aloides (Water Soldier)

Lysimachlia nummularla

Sagittaria sagittifolia

Myriophyllum proserpinacoides (Parrots feather)

Water Hawthorn *(Aponogeton distachyos)* comes from South Africa. Not totally hardy and therefore needs to be planted a minimum of 40cm (15in) deep to avoid any freezing. It suffers from water snails.

For those of you with smaller ponds, it is a chance to give an impression of a larger wet area than there is in reality. In the vicinity of the pond, plants such as *Iris sibirica*, *Hostas*, *Houttynias*, *Lobelia cardinalis* and Mimulus are just some that can extend the herbaceous border right to the pool edge. Combined with Primula and Ferns, Astilbes, Ligularia and the like, you extend the boundaries of the damp patch as well as the seasons of interest.

Many marginals are spring flowering, so maintain your interest for the rest of the season with some variegated varieties and an assortment of leaf shape and plant form. There are variegated forms of Sweet Flag *(Acorus calamus variegata)*, a yellow clumping rush is Carex 'Bowles Gold', and the popular Yellow Flag, *Iris pseudacorus*, has a variegated form. A bit of a conversation piece is the 'zebra striped rush' *Scirpus zebrinus*, which has horizontal stripes. For a bright splash of lush variegated foliage, there is nothing to beat *Scrophularia auriculata variegata* (Water Figwort), with its large, soft, sage-like leaves.

Pruning and replanting marginal plants

Cut back plant. Save some exterior growth. It may be better than the plant material in the basket, if the plant centre seems exhausted.

Remove plant from the basket and divide it with the two forks method.

Line the basket with new hessian liner.

Old planting baskets with overgrown plant removed from the pond. Excess growth from around the outside is cut away.

Smaller clumps can be split by hand.

Remove fresh new growth from old stock.

Collect several new shoots that show rooting.

Fill with aquatic soil mix. Tuck in excess hessian. Push in shoots at the angle they would seem to grow with the roots down into the compost/soil. The shoots should be just showing at the soil surface.

Top off with a layer of pea shingle, making sure the shoot tips still show.

Place as soon as possible in the pool at the required level.

The Lythrums are one of the few later-flowering graces together with the very sedate Arum Lily *(Zantedeschia aethiopica)* or the Bog Arum *(Calla palustris)* or the very similar but larger Skunk Cabbage *(Lysichiton americanum)*. *Lobelia cardinalis*, with its dark-red foliage and bright-red flower, makes a striking sight if it has survived the ravages of snail and wind. After this, in early August, you must turn to the lilies in the deep water department for your floral entertainment.

Instead of planting in rows, try to get some depth to the planting even on the marginal shelf by having some plants in front of others. Then try using the ground cover qualities of plants such as Brooklime, Parrots Feather, Creeping Jenny and Mimulus to run through the baskets as cover and basket disguise.

A water garden is not a particularly low-maintenance part of the garden. You may not have to mow it every week like the lawn, and most of the time it only needs an eye kept on it. But when there *is* work to be done, it is a *lot* of work, and generally at the worst time of year. It is your choice to have a water garden and any work you do will prove more profitable if it is done with forethought and with a grander scheme in mind than simply to have a row of sorry soldiers trying to stand to attention around the pool.

Handy Hints for Choosing Suitable Marginal Plants

1.   Do not accept hand-outs of marginals unless they come with written guarantees that they won't take over your pond in what seems like less than five minutes.
2.   If you have a small pond, beware of cheap plants, especially if they are big and being sold in clumps. Water plants seem to grow in inverse proportion to their relative cost.
3.   Make sure you have properly identified the plant you are putting in your pool. If you bought it in a retail outlet, was it properly labelled? Several of the rushes look remarkably alike in their infancy but, as they grow older, some take to vandalising the liner as though it was gossamer. Nothing stands in their way.
4.   Try to see what the plant looks like in a mature clump, that is, at 3–4 years old. Will it be too tall? Is the form suitable for the position you have in mind for it? When adult, it may have more to recommend it than just the flower.
5.   You will find that the more specialised varieties of plants, although quite capable of looking after their own needs, may require a certain amount of protection from bullying neighbours.
6.   Some non-indigenous varieties do need frost protection for the winter, for example, *Lobelia cardinalis* and Arum Lilies.
7.   Your choice of plants will naturally depend upon the style of planting you have chosen, with native plants for a natural or wild garden, colour and form for a more ornamental planting. However, unless you are after something that creates a very formal atmosphere, as with an occasional clump of very upright Irises, then a mixture of habitat, form, leaf shape and colour is essential in the choice of plants.
8.   Many plants are worth collecting just for their names. Who can fail to be impressed when you ascribe humble, innocuous flora with appellations such as *Butomus umbellatus, Lysimachia nummularia, Myosotis scorpioides, Myriophyllum proserpinacoides* or even *Veronica beccabunga?*

Propagating and Dividing Marginal Plants

If you have ever divided up herbaceous plants on dry land, then you will be familiar with the operation of dividing up the mass of rhizomes, tubers or stolons with two garden forks back to back. Alternatively, try to tease it apart gently by hand or launch a brutal attack with spade and knife to divide the lively new growth on the outside from the tangled, choked-up mass in the centre.

Most marginal plants respond vigorously. You should bear this in mind if you feel tempted to mix them by planting different types in the same container. They will soon run all over each other and one will become dominant at the expense of the others.

Vigour and the ability to spread by seed and root run riot in the marginal plant world. But what gives some of them the 'upper petiole', so to speak, is root exudes. These are chemical growth inhibitors that decrease the competition from surrounding water plants. This is another good reason not to put one type of plant in with another.

If in doubt as to what will survive when dividing up an old clump, take what seems to be a substantial proportion of the most recent regrowth and replant it at the same level in the soil that it was at previously. Replant it in the same type of compost that you would use for the Lilies. Top dress with gravel in the same way. Make sure any fresh emergent shoots are not buried under the gravel and compost and can get a look at the sun.

Placing marginal plants in their baskets in the pond is a relatively easy operation done from the bank. As a general rule, the plants will all be quite happy if the water is just over the edge of the planting basket by little more than half an inch. You may need to raise the baskets up on flat stones. Perhaps if some baskets sit a little too deeply in the water, you could reserve these for the *Alisma* (Plantain), *Calla* (Bogbean), *Orontium* (Golden Club), *Pontederia* (Pickerel), *Sagittaria* (Arrowhead) and *Typha latifolia* (Reed Mace). All these plants can be submerged from 5–10cm (2–4in). *Zantedeschia* (Arum Lily) appreciates a depth of 15–23cm (6–9in).

Floating Plants

Just throw them in as soon as possible after getting them. Don't be disappointed if they sink; they will soon sort themselves out. Water Soldier and Frogbit sink in the winter anyway and come up as the water warms in spring.

Fairy Moss *(Azolla coronilla)*, Water Hyacinth *(Eichornia crassipes)* and Water Lettuce *(Pistia stratiotes)* are frost-tender and need to be overwintered indoors. A stock of *Azolla* can be overwintered in a small pan of loam and water. The Hyacinth and Lettuce can be planted in some damp, fertiliser-free, fibrous loam or compost.

Oxygenators

If you want the most efficient oxygenator, buy *Elodea crispa*, usually referred to in books as *Lagarosiphon major*. This can be rampant, but it does the job and can be kept in check easily. Don't get palmed off with Canadian Pondweed *(Elodea canadensis)*, sometimes referred to as Anacharis or Water Thyme. In a freshly established, nutrient-rich pond this is really rampant. However, on the plus side, I do find it quite effective when planted almost at water level in the same basket as some vigorous reeds. Here it provides an effective green carpet that works as useful marginal ground cover.

Whatever you choose will be sold in bunches held together with lead wire. This wire may be heavy enough to sink the bunch if it is just dropped in. If you did this, the weed would probably send out roots quite quickly and effectively, but ultimately you will find it best to establish a properly-planted group that can be cut and trimmed to size in relation to the point at which it is anchored. If you have to hack into a mass of weed with no

Taking cuttings to propagate and revitalise oxygenators.

Snip off tips or sections of oxygenator.

Bunch 4 or 5 10cm (4in) lengths (you can keep them together with lead wire).

Push the bunches of oxygenator into a basket full of pea shingle. In an established pond they will rapidly root in this medium.

Place in the pond as soon as possible at a depth of approximately 30cm (12in) below the surface of the water until the plants seems to be in full growth. Then they can be replaced at the bottom of the pond.

beginning and no end, you find yourself pulling most of it out in one long strand, and any still in the pool is left floating on the top.

Propagating and Planting Oxygenators

All oxygenating weed gets straggly and out of hand. Just cutting it back encourages the plants to shoot from bare stems near the point of anchorage or rooting. There comes a point, however, especially when you are having a major clean out, when it is advisable and often necessary to establish new colonies of oxygenating weed. The raw material is the fresh growing tips of the plants. These must be kept moist at all times. Collect tips 10–12cm (4–5in) in length in bunches of five or six and push these into a planting basket full of pea gravel. It is not absolutely necessary to have soil in the basket although some say it helps to get the plant established more quickly.

Place the basket in its position under water as soon as possible. To begin with, the maximum depth should be no more than 46cm (18in).

Newly-Established Ponds

Depending when and where you have created your water garden, it may seem that many plants take a long time to get established. If you have been able to fulfil all the correct criteria with regard to siting, establishment and stock levels (see Chapter 2), it may be simply due to the weather. Water plants, in common with all other plants, need prescribed levels of light, water, nutrition and temperature in order to thrive.

Causes of plant problems in newly-established ponds.

1. Minimum 4 hours' sun a day and protection from the north and prevailing winds. Too much heat and sun can cause algae problems in the early days. Don't change the water, don't use algicides.
2. Plants at the right depth.
3. Temperature right for the time of year.
4. Nutritional problems.
5. Grazing Koi carp.
6. Grazing snails.

1. Marginals and lilies need as much sunlight as possible in order to flower, and oxygenators need it to photosynthesise and produce oxygen. Any sort of shade upsets this to a very large degree.

2. A prescribed depth of water in which to grow is essential for happy marginal plants and lilies, although some marginals are extremely adaptable to dry conditions and some lilies are encouraged to flower extremely profusely in half their normal planting depth. It is change, particularly regular change in water depth, that will not be tolerated.

3.   Change in temperature also upsets water plants. Although the biological clock in most marginal plants makes them 'early risers' in the spring and they seem to plod on in the most miserable conditions, a sudden change in temperature from mild southerlies to a cool north wind can soon blacken them off. Just minor changes in temperature can produce a check in growth, which is when the grey mould of mildew can arise opportunistically on Marsh Marigolds and Forget-me-nots.

Marsh Marigolds, the tips of Irises and Bog Arums easily fall prey to frosts. Although the well-established plants recover when they 'come again', freshly-established plants, standing alone and vulnerable without the resources and protection afforded by a group planting, easily succumb. Combine this with the added possibility that many marginal plants sold for retail in garden centres are 'brought on' in greenhouses and polytunnels to take advantage of the early season sales. It is then no wonder that newly-planted water gardens get mown flat by the late spring frosts.

4.   Any fertiliser that is available to a newly-planted water plant will only be used if the above conditions are right. Slow-release fertiliser in the planting basket only becomes a pollutant. On the other hand, even if these conditions are right, growth cannot be expected unless some nutrition is available. There may not be much in the fresh water and it may be that only once there is a fully-established cycle of life in the pond will naturally-occurring nitrates be available to plants. A bucket of water from an established healthy pond, 'Pond Start' chemicals and the introduction of fish all help to get things going.

5.   Big, bored fish, especially carp if they are introduced into the pool too early, can be a menace as they grub around in lily baskets until the tubers float to the surface.

6.   Water snails introduced into newly-established ponds too early can cause havoc as well.

Established Ponds

Aquatic plants, both deep water or marginals, need splitting up every 3–5 years, depending on the size of the pond. Small set-ups may need an annual trim and sort out. The centres of clumps of marginals may seem lifeless with all the fresh growth outside the basket. In this case, replant, discarding the centre (see *Plant Division and Propagation*).

General Plant Problems

Aphids or Blackfly
1.   Rub off plants or spray with a jet of water. Fish will eat them.
2.   Be very careful with insecticides. Systemic insecticides might be possible if you can avoid getting too much in the water. One expert recommends spraying the plants with a fish parasite treatment if sensitive orfe or rudd are not present. Prepare the chemical at the recommended dose for pond treatment and spray on.

Blackened Foliage
1.   Either late frosts or inclement wind from an exposed direction. Established plants will grow into recovery. Most marginal plants store a lot of growth potential in rhizomes or tubers.
2.   Too much medication, in particular salt. A water change is essential.

Distorted Foliage
Aphids, chills or snails (see above and *Snails*).

Eaten Foliage and General Plant Pests
Brown China Moth: See *Pests and Diseases to Specific Plants: Water Lilies* below.
Caddis flies: Caddis fly larvae feed on submerged foliage and cut pieces out of water lily leaves. The best control is fish, particularly tench.
Snails: Snails do great damage to all plants, particularly submerged ones. Eggs look like toothpaste-size extrusions of clear or dotted silicon on the underside of leaves, particularly lilies. Rub them off. Fish will eat some snails' eggs. To get rid of the snails themselves, dangle a cabbage stump in the water and they will flock to it. Grapefruit rind or lettuce leaves are also suggested lures to entrap them.
Water Lily Beetle: See *Pests and Diseases to Specific Plants: Water Lilies* below.

Pests and Diseases to Specific Plants

Water Lilies
Brown China Moth *(Hydrocampa nymphaeata)*: This small brown and orange moth lays clusters of eggs on water lily leaves in summer. Larvae feed on the leaves and hide from view between two pieces of leaf that they stick together. Pick off affected leaves or submerge them to be dealt with by the fish.
Crown Rot: Covers a number of fungal and bacterial diseases. Mottled leafed varieties are particularly affected; for example, Root Rot affects the Yellows *moorei* and *chromatella*. Symptoms generally include the leaves turning yellow and black, and these are easily pulled away from the centre crown. Eventually the crown begins to rot.
   The solution is to remove the lily and cut away the diseased tissue. Recovery may come from other growing points. Spray with systemic fungicide and quarantine until strong growth is visible. This normally occurs on newly-planted stock. Therefore, don't plant new plants too deep and beware of sudden chills.
Leaf Spots: With *Cercosporae*, edges of the leaves become dry and crumbly. *Ovularia nymphaeum* causes small spots that readily spread, after which the leaves rot in patches. Pick off affected leaves and burn. If the plant is heavily infested, the careful use of a systemic fungicide may be in order.
Water Lily Beetle *(Galerucella nymphaea)*: Larvae and adults feed on the leaves and flowers. Spray with a forceful jet of water. The dislodged pests will be eaten by the fish. If no fish are present, then spray very carefully with a systemic insecticide. An alternative suggestion is to spray with fish parasite solution at a dose rate suitable for the pool.
Water Lily Midge: The leaves of smaller varieties of water lily are reduced to skeletons by small midge larvae working in from the edge. Treat as for Water Lily Beetle (above).

Marginals
Caltha (Marsh Marigold): All varieties are prone to mildew and fungal infections. Generally it occurs as a matter of course at the end of the flowering period. It can be treated in isolation with systemic fungicide. Alternatively, simply pick off infected leaves.
Houttuynia cordata plena is prone to scorching by late frosts.
Myosotis palustris (Water Forget-me-not): This is prone to mildew at the end of the flowering season. Leave until it sets some seed and cut right back or pull up.

Some water plant afflictions.

Leaf spot diseases.

Spots developing into holes.

Elodea (oxygenator) encrusted with lime from fresh limey water.

Lily pad showing evidence of Brown China Moth grubs in residence.

Water Lily Midge damage.

Lily pad and flower damage by the Water Lily Beetle.

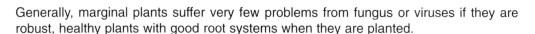

Generally, marginal plants suffer very few problems from fungus or viruses if they are robust, healthy plants with good root systems when they are planted.

Floating Plants

Disappearance: Frogbit and Water Soldier will sink to the bottom of the pool as the water gets colder. They will also disappear in cool weather after some major upheaval or disturbance.

Water Chestnut is an annual and will only reappear after winter if it has managed to set seed. This does not occur very often. If it does set seed, sow in pans of loam in water in April or May. Heat to around 18–21°C (64–70°F) until germination occurs, then grow on in a unheated greenhouse.

Blackened foliage: From greenhouse to pool is a dangerous time for Water Hyacinth *(Eichornia crassipes)* or Water Lettuce *(Pistia stratiotes)*. Even the slightest frost can spell doom.

Oxygenators

Brown or white crusty scale: Hard water or lime in the water. Rub off, particularly around the growing tips. Do a pH test for a possible water change or buffer chemical to make the water more acid.

Disappearance: Usually caused by snails or carp. Blame the bloke in the shop who said these were a good idea.

BIBLIOGRAPHY

The Completely Illustrated Guide to Koi for your Pond by Dr. Herbert R. Axelrod, Balon, Hoffman, Rothbard and Wohlfarth.
TFH Publications Inc.

Brookes, Alan and Agate, Elizabeth, *Waterways and Wetlands*, (BTCV).
Heritage, Bill, *Ponds and Water Gardens*. He is *the* man.
Macan, T T and Worthington-Collins, E B, *Life in Lakes and Rivers*
May, Peter, *The Perfect Pond Recipe Book*.
May, Peter, *The Perfect Pond Detective Book 2: Physical and Mechanical Problems*.
Palmer, C Mervin, *Algae and Water Pollution*
Perry, Frances, *Water Gardens*. She is *the* lady.

All serious pond owners should subscribe to *The Water Gardener Magazine, Practical Fishkeeping* and *Aquarist and Pond Keeper* readily available from newsagents.

Every pond owner should have the *Observer's Book of Pond Life* by John Clegg, first published by Warne in 1956.

CONVERSION TABLES

Length

1 inch	=	25.4 millimetres	1 millimetre	=	0.0394 inches
1 inch	=	2.54 centimetres	1 centimetre	=	0.394 inches
1 foot	=	30.5 centimetres	1 metre	=	39.4 inches
1 foot	=	0.305 metres	1 metre	=	3.28 feet
1 yard	=	0.914 metres	1 metre	=	1.09 yards
1 mile	=	0.609 kilometres	kilometre	=	0.621 miles

Weight

1 ounce	=	28.3 grams	1 gram	=	0.035 ounces
1 pound	=	454 grams	1 kilogram	=	2.2 pounds
1 pound	=	0.454 kilograms	1 metric tonne	=	2200 pounds
1 ton	=	1.02 metric tonnes	1 metric tonne	=	0.984 tons

Capacity

1 fluid ounce	=	28.4 millilitres	1 millilitre	=	0.035 fluid ounces
1 pint	=	0.568 litres	1 litre	=	1.76 pints
1 UK gallon	=	4.55 litres	1 litre	=	0.22 UK gallons
1 UK gallon	=	1.2 US gallons	1 US gallon	=	0.833 UK gallons

Area

1 sq in	=	6.45 sq centimetres	1 sq centimetre	=	0.155 sq inches
1 sq foot	=	929 sq centimetres	1 sq metre	=	10.76 sq feet
1 sq foot	=	0.093 sq metres	1 sq metre	=	1.2 sq yard
1 sq yard	=	0.836 sq metres	1 hectare	=	2.47 acres
1 acre	=	0.405 hectares	1 sq kilometre	=	247 acres
1 sq mile	=	259 hectares	1 sq kilometre	=	0.386 sq miles
1 sq mile	=	2.59 sq kilometres			

Volume

1 cu inch	=	16.4 cu centimetres	1 cu centimetre	=	0.061 cu inches
1 cu foot	=	0.028 cu metres	1 cu metre	=	35.3 cu feet
1 cu yard	=	0.765 cu metres	1 cu metre	=	1.31 cu yards

Abbreviations

centimetre(s)	=	cm
foot, feet	=	ft
gram(s)	=	g
inch(es)	=	in
kilogram(s)	=	kg
metre(s)	=	m
millimetre(s)	=	mm
ounce(s)	=	oz
pound(s)	=	lb
litre(s)	=	l

INDEX